Contents

Contents

CAMBRIDGE
UNIVERSITY PRESS

CAMBRIDGE
Primary Mathematics

Workbook 3

Cherri Moseley & Janet Rees

CAMBRIDGE
UNIVERSITY PRESS

University Printing House, Cambridge CB2 8BS, United Kingdom

One Liberty Plaza, 20th Floor, New York, NY 10006, USA

477 Williamstown Road, Port Melbourne, VIC 3207, Australia

314–321, 3rd Floor, Plot 3, Splendor Forum, Jasola District Centre, New Delhi – 110025, India

103 Penang Road, #05–06/07, Visioncrest Commercial, Singapore 238467

Cambridge University Press is part of the University of Cambridge.

It furthers the University's mission by disseminating knowledge in the pursuit of education, learning and research at the highest international levels of excellence.

www.cambridge.org
Information on this title: www.cambridge.org/9781108746496

First published 2014
Second edition 2021

20 19 18 17 16 15 14 13 12 11 10 9 8 7

Printed in India by Multivista Global Pvt Ltd

A catalogue record for this publication is available from the British Library

ISBN 978-1-108-74649-6 Paperback with Digital Access (1 Year)

Additional resources for this publication at www.cambridge.org/9781108746496

How to use this book

This workbook provides questions for you to practise what you have learned in class. There is a unit to match each unit in your Learner's Book. Each exercise is divided into three parts:

- **Focus:** these questions help you to master the basics
- **Practice:** these questions help you to become more confident in using what you have learned
- **Challenge:** these questions will make you think more deeply.

You might not need to work on all three parts of each exercise. Your teacher will tell you which parts to do.

You will also find these features:

Important words that ⟶ you will use.

Step-by-step examples showing a way to solve a problem. ⟶

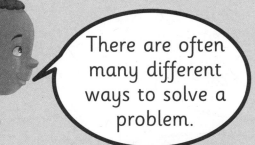
There are often many different ways to solve a problem.

These questions will help you develop your skills of thinking ⟶ and working mathematically.

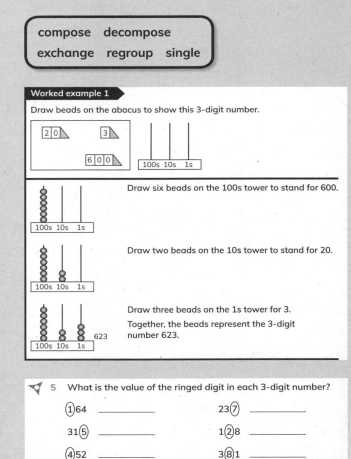

compose   decompose
exchange   regroup   single

Worked example 1

Draw beads on the abacus to show this 3-digit number.

| 2 0 | | 3 |
| | 6 0 0 |

100s 10s 1s

Draw six beads on the 100s tower to stand for 600.

100s 10s 1s

Draw two beads on the 10s tower to stand for 20.

100s 10s 1s

Draw three beads on the 1s tower for 3.
Together, the beads represent the 3-digit number 623.

100s 10s 1s   623

5   What is the value of the ringed digit in each 3-digit number?

①64 _____   23⑦ _____

31⑤ _____   1②8 _____

④52 _____   3⑧1 _____

Thinking and Working Mathematically

There are some important skills that you will develop as you learn mathematics.

Specialising
is when I choose an example and check to see if it satisfies or does not satisfy specific mathematical criteria.

Characterising
is when I identify and describe the mathematical properties of an object.

Generalising
is when I recognise an underlying pattern by identifying many examples that satisfy the same mathematical criteria.

Classifying
is when I organise objects into groups according to their mathematical properties.

Critiquing is when I compare and evaluate mathematical ideas, representations or solutions to identify advantages and disadvantages.

Improving is when I refine mathematical ideas or representations to develop a more effective approach or solution.

Conjecturing is when I form mathematical questions or ideas.

Convincing is when I present evidence to justify or challenge a mathematical idea or solution.

1 ▶ Numbers to 1000

> 1.1 Hundreds, tens and ones

Exercise 1.1

Focus

1 Here is the last row of a 100 square. Write the numbers in the next row, which is the first row of the 101 to 200 square.

91	92	93	94	95	96	97	98	99	100
101									

2 Complete these pieces from a 1 to 1000 number strip.

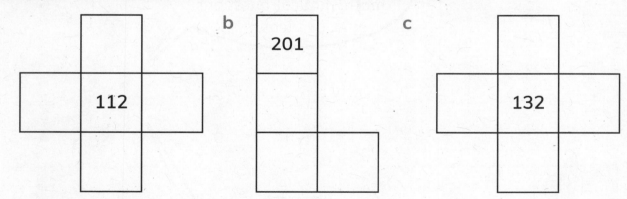

3 Draw a representation of 316.
   How will you show the value of each digit?

Now write this number in words.

_____

4 What 3-digit numbers are represented below?

a

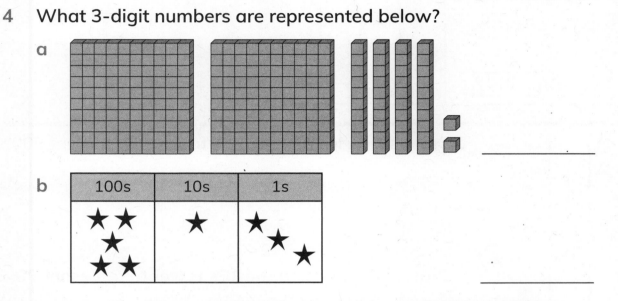

_____

b

100s	10s	1s
★ ★ ★ ★ ★	★	★ ★ ★

_____

5 What is the value of the ringed digit in each 3-digit number?

①64 _____   23⑦ _____

31⑤ _____   1②8 _____

④52 _____   3⑧1 _____

Which hundreds values have not been used in these numbers?

_____

Practice

6 Write the numbers in the next row of the 1 to 1000 strip.

351	352	353	354	355	356	357	358	359	360

Worked example 1

Draw beads on the abacus to show this 3-digit number.

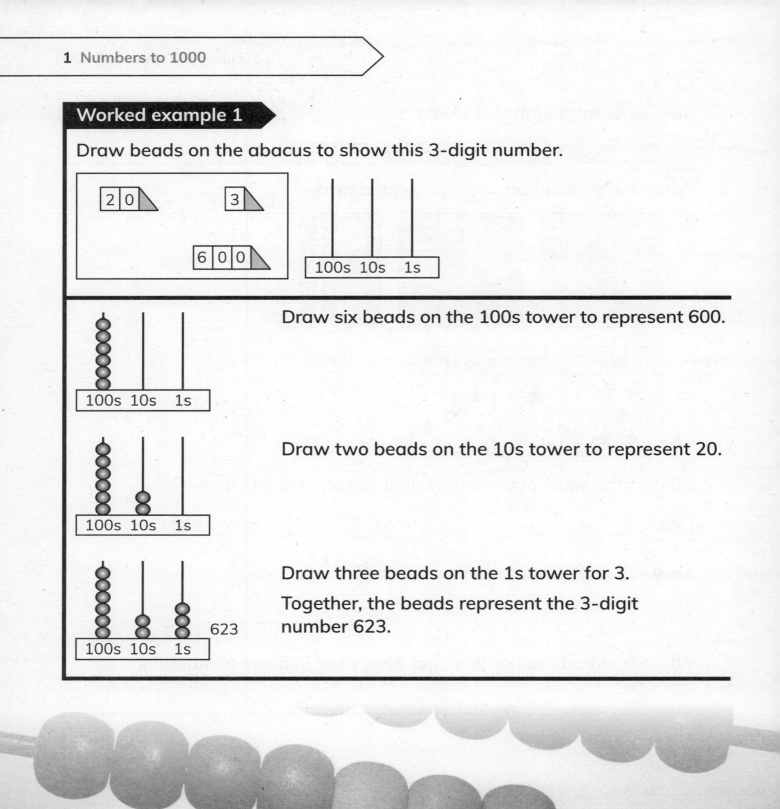

Draw six beads on the 100s tower to represent 600.

Draw two beads on the 10s tower to represent 20.

Draw three beads on the 1s tower for 3.

Together, the beads represent the 3-digit number 623.

7   Draw beads on each abacus to represent each 3-digit number.

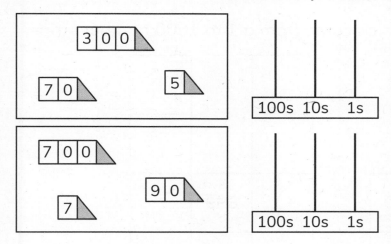

8   Which 3-digit number is represented on each abacus? Write each number in words.

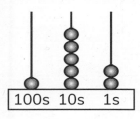

_____

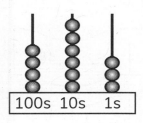

_____

9   Write this 3-digit number in words.

100	200	300	400	500	600	700	800	900
10	20	30	40	50	60	70	80	90
1	2	3	4	5	6	7	8	9

_____

Challenge

10 Complete these pieces, which come from a 1 to 1000 number strip.

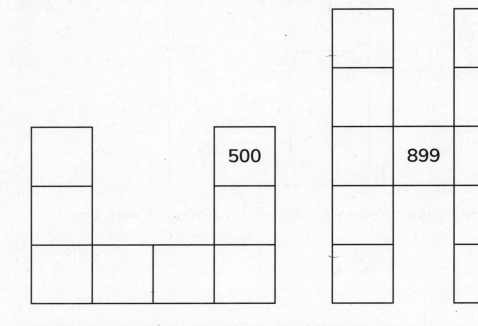

11 Write the missing numbers on each worm.

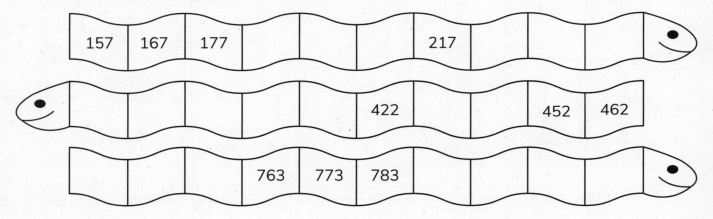

12

> When you have two different digit cards, you can make two different 2-digit numbers. So when you have three different digit cards, you must be able to make three different 3-digit numbers.

Is Arun correct? How do you know?

_____

_____

13   Read along each row to find three 3-digit numbers.

5	4	6
3	1	8
9	7	2

Read down each column to find another three 3-digit numbers.

Write each number in words.

_____

_____

_____

_____

_____

_____

> 1.2 Comparing and ordering

Exercise 1.2

| inequality | is greater than, > |
| is less than, < |

Focus

1   Complete these pieces, which come from a 1000 strip.

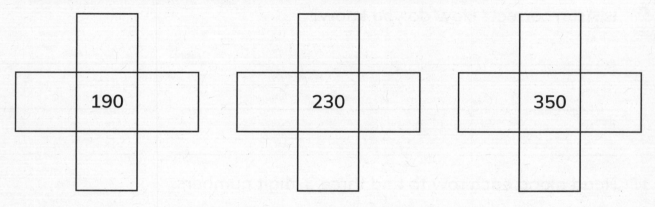

2   Compare these numbers and complete the sentences.

100s	10s	1s
2	4	9
1	7	3

_____ is less than _____ and

_____ is greater than _____.

3   Write the statements in question 2 using the symbols < and >.

_____

_____

4 Order these numbers from smallest to greatest.

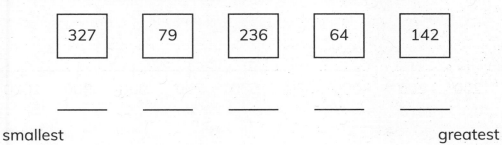

_____   _____   _____   _____   _____

smallest   greatest

5 Estimate the value of each number marked on the number line.

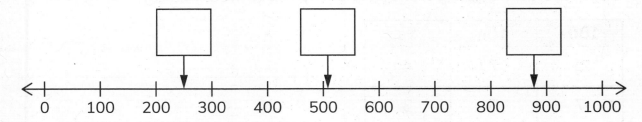

Practice

6 Use < and > to write two inequalities about these numbers.

100s	10s	1s
4	5	6
4	6	5

_____

_____

7 Order these numbers from greatest to smallest.

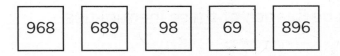

_____   _____   _____   _____   _____

greatest   smallest

8 Mark the numbers from question 7 on the number line.

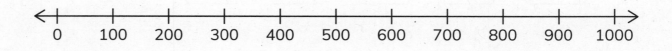

Challenge

9 Compare these numbers. Write some inequalities using < or >.

100s	10s	1s
5	7	4
7	5	3
5	4	7

_____

_____

_____

10 Yusef looks at the place value grid in question 9 and writes:

547 < 753 > 574   753 > 547 < 574

Write some more inequalities like those written by Yusef.

_____

11 What could the missing digit be in each of these inequalities?

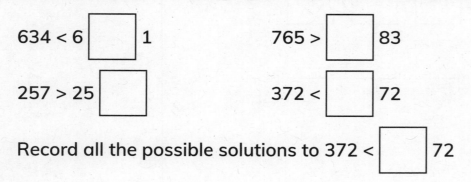

634 < 6 ☐ 1   765 > ☐ 83

257 > 25 ☐   372 < ☐ 72

Record all the possible solutions to 372 < ☐ 72

_____

12 Order the heights of these towers from shortest to tallest.

Name of tower	Location	Height in metres
Lakhta Centre	St Petersburg	462
Willis Tower	Chicago	442
Burj Khalifa	Dubai	828
Petronas Tower 1	Kuala Lumpur	452
Shanghai Tower	Shanghai	632
Lotte World Tower	Seoul	555

Heights in metres:

_____   _____   _____   _____   _____   _____

  shortest   tallest

13 Write the digits 1 to 9 anywhere in the grid.

Read across and down the grid to find six 3-digit numbers.
Mark each number on the number line.

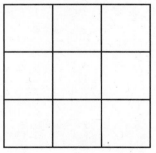

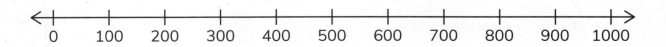

> 1.3 Estimating and rounding

Exercise 1.3

Focus

1 Estimate how many dots there are in the box.

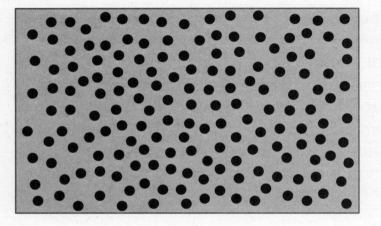

estimate   range
round, rounding

2 Estimate how many grains of rice are on the middle spoon.

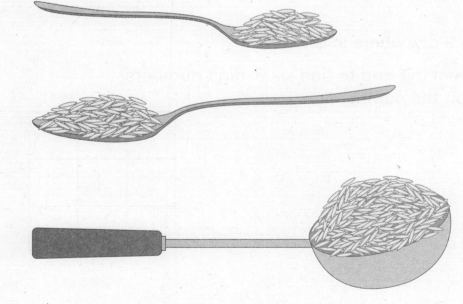

estimate: 100 – 200

estimate: _____

estimate: 400 – 600

3   Round each number to the nearest 10.

271 _____   138 _____

397 _____   404 _____

4   Round each number to the nearest 100.

164 _____   325 _____

449 _____   250 _____

Practice

5   Class 3 used this table to make estimates of the
    number of grains in different plastic bags.

Mass of grains	Number of grains	Mass of grains	Number of grains
5 grams	100	30 grams	600
10 grams	200	35 grams	700
15 grams	300	40 grams	800
20 grams	400	45 grams	900
25 grams	500	50 grams	1000

a   Samira estimates that her plastic bag had 300 to 400 grains.
    They weighed 18 grams. Is this a good estimate?

    _____

b   Pedro's grains weighed 31 grams.
    What range would be a good estimate for his grains?

    _____

6 Round each amount to the nearest $10.

$537 _____ $772 _____

$695 _____ $808 _____

7 Round each amount to the nearest 100 kilograms.

150 kilograms _____ kilograms

555 kilograms _____ kilograms

444 kilograms _____ kilograms

501 kilograms _____ kilograms

Challenge

8   Round the height of each tower to the nearest 10 metres
    and to the nearest 100 metres.

Name of tower	Location	Height in metres	Nearest 10 metres	Nearest 100 metres
Lakhta Centre	St Petersburg	462		
Willis Tower	Chicago	442		
Burj Khalifa	Dubai	828		
Petronas Tower 1	Kuala Lumpur	452		
Shanghai Tower	Shanghai	632		
Lotte World Tower	Seoul	555		

9   Which towers round to the same height when their heights are
    rounded to the nearest 100 metres?

    _____

    _____

10 Zara rounds a number to the nearest 10 and to the
    nearest 100. Her answer both times is 500.
    What could her number be? Record all the possible answers.

11 Follow the rounding instructions.
    What do you notice about the results of rounding to 100?

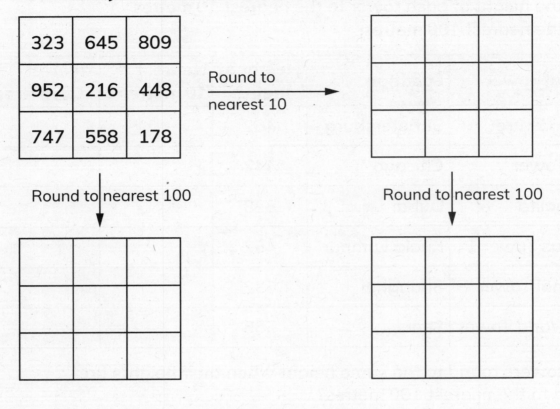

323	645	809
952	216	448
747	558	178

Round to nearest 10 →

Round to nearest 100 ↓

Round to nearest 100 ↓

_____

_____

12 In a shop, all prices are rounded to the nearest $10.
    Would all the customers be happy about the changes in price?
    Explain your answer.

_____

_____

2 ▶ Statistics: tally charts and frequency tables

> ## > 2.1 Tally charts and frequency tables

Exercise 2.1

frequency table

survey

Focus

1   Tom produces a tally chart showing 17 triangles, 25 squares, 9 pentagons and 24 circles.

Complete his chart.

Shape	Tally
○	
□	
△	
⬠	

a   What is the total number of shapes? _____

b   Which shape has the highest total? _____

c   Which shape has the lowest total? _____

d   Which two shapes have a total frequency of 42? _____

2   Use the tally chart in question 1 to make a frequency table.
    Draw the shapes.

Shape	Frequency

3   a   Fill in the missing parts of this table.

Ways to travel to school

Ways of travelling	Tally	Frequency
walk		12
bike	ⅢⅢ ‖‖	
bus		6
car	‖‖	

b   Which way of traveling to school is the most popular?

_____

c   How many learners travel to school in total? _____

4   You have been asked to help plan a party.

Which part will you help with? You could choose the food, the drinks, the music or a choice of your own.

_____

You are going to investigate what the most popular options are.

Write a question that you will ask people. Give them four different options.

_____

_____

Now you need to ask your question to up to ten people. Record your data below.

> **Tip**
>
> Think about how you will record your data. Remember to add any labels or headings.

Write three sentences about the data you collected.

1 _____

2 _____

3 _____

Explain what you will choose for the party and why.

_____

_____

Practice

5   Complete the tally chart to show the numbers of vertices
    in each shape.

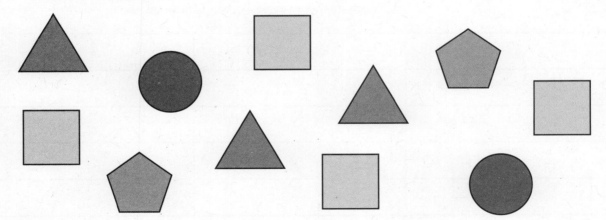

Number of vertices	Tally
0	
1	
2	
3	
4	
5	

Write three different things that the tally chart shows you.

1 _____

2 _____

3 _____

6   This frequency table shows the number of sweets in 20 bags.

Number of sweets	Frequency
23	1
24	4
25	9
26	3
27	3

Use the data in the frequency table to write three questions for your partner.

1 _____

2 _____

3 _____

7   This table shows the colour of the cars parked outside
    the school.

white	purple	black	purple	black	green
red	green	blue	white	purple	white
yellow	blue	white	blue	black	green
green	yellow	blue	yellow	black	blue

Complete the table to show the car colours.

Colour	white	blue	black	red	yellow	green	purple
Tally							
Frequency							

Write three questions about the data in the table for
your partner to answer.

1 _____

2 _____

3 _____

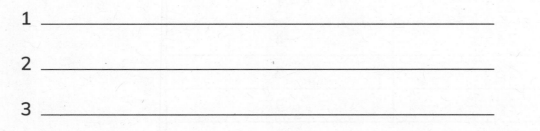

8 You have been asked to help design a new park in your local town. You can only choose one attraction for the park.

Write a question that you will ask people. Give them different options to choose from.

_____

_____

_____

Now you need to ask your question to up to ten people. Record your data below.

> **Tip**
>
> Think about how you will record your data. Remember to add any labels or headings.

Write three sentences about the data you collected.

1 _____

2 _____

3 _____

Explain what you will choose for the park and why.

_____

_____

How could you improve your investigation?

_____

_____

Challenge

9   Nasif does a survey. He asks his classmates what kind of pet they have. He records the data like this.

Pets	Tally	Frequency
cat	ⵜⵜⵜ ⵜⵜⵜ ⵜⵜⵜ ⵜⵜⵜ		26
fish	ⵜⵜⵜ |||	8
rabbit	||||	4
horse	||||	3
other	ⵜⵜⵜ ⵜⵜⵜ	10
	Total	**47**

Nasif has made three mistakes in the Frequency column. Find his mistakes and correct them.

10 Trang is ill and cannot go to school. She counts and records the number of people in cars travelling down her street in 2 hours.

Number of people in each car	Number of cars
1	41
2	54
3	32
4	20
5	3

a How many cars went past Trang's house? _____

b How many people in total travelled in those cars? _____

11 Zara records the results of a survey of the most popular rides
    at the funfair from 3 p.m. to 4 p.m.

    a   Zara spills some ink on her table. Can you help her fill in the gaps?

Ride	Tally	Frequency
carousel	卌 卌 卌 III	
bumper cars	卌 卌 卌	
Ferris wheel		23
helter skelter		14
roller coaster		28
teacups	卌 卌 II	
waltzers		21
drop tower	卌 卌 卌 卌 卌 卌 I	
pirate ship		27

    b   Write three questions for your partner to answer.

        1 _____

        2 _____

        3 _____

12 Your school is putting on an event to raise money for charity.
    You have been asked to help plan the event.

    How could you investigate what event to hold?

    _____

    _____

Write a question that you will ask people. Give them different options to choose from.

_____

_____

_____

Ask your question to up to ten people. Record your data below.

Write three sentences about the data you collected.

1 _____

2 _____

3 _____

Explain what you will choose for the event and why.

_____

_____

Write two other questions you could investigate to help
with your planning.

_____

_____

How could you improve your investigation?

_____

_____

3 ▶ Addition, subtraction and money

> 3.1 Addition

Exercise 3.1

compose	decompose
exchange	regroup single

Focus

1 Complete each addition. Show how you found each total.

$24 + 5$

$=$

$42 + 5$

$=$

$48 + 9$

$=$

$37 + 8$

$=$

2 Complete each addition. Show how you found each total.

$123 + 6$

$=$

$153 + 5$

$=$

$254 + 7$

$=$

$235 + 8$

$=$

3   Estimate and then complete each addition to find the total.

112 + 26 =   estimate =

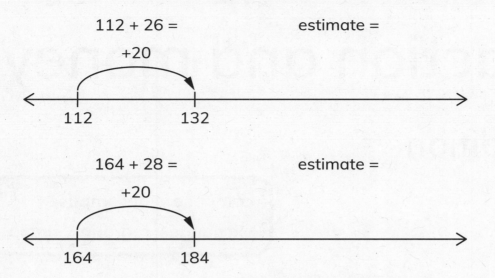

164 + 28 =   estimate =

4   Cheng did not have enough time to finish his calculations.
    Complete them both for him.

a   315 + 232   estimate: 320 + 230 = 550

    = 300 + 10 + 5 + 200 + 30 + 2

    =

b   247 + 218   estimate: 250 + 220 =

    = 200 + 40 + 7 +

    =

Practice

5   Read across or down the grid to find a 2-digit number.
     Add six to each number. Show how you found your totals.

4	3
7	8

6   Complete each addition. Show how you found each total.

$246 + 3$ $171 + 7$

$=$ $=$

$345 + 8$ $269 + 9$

$=$ $=$

7   The baker makes 246 small cakes and 26 large cakes.
     How many cakes does the baker make all together?

     Estimate and then find the total. Show your method.

8   A market stall has 38 apples left.
    A box of 148 apples are delivered.
    How many apples are on
    the stall now?

    Estimate, then calculate.
    Show your method.

9   359 children and 218 adults
    visited the play park today.
    How many people visited the
    play park today?

    Estimate and then calculate.
    Show your method.

10 Estimate the total, then use an empty number line to help
    you add 414 and 268.

Challenge

11 The addition machine adds 56 to each number in the grid.

Estimate and then complete the answer grid.
How will you find the totals?

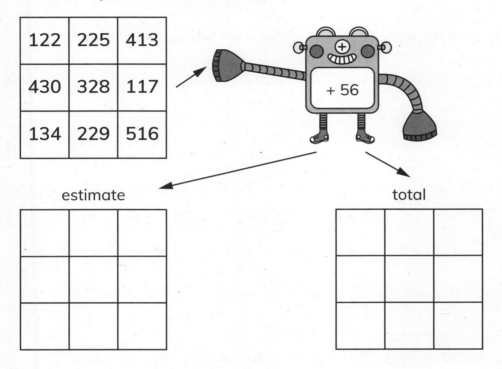

122	225	413
430	328	117
134	229	516

+ 56

estimate

total

12 Angela spilt some ink on the ones digits in her number sentence.

32 ⬤ + 14 ⬤ = 475

What could her calculation have been? Find all the possible answers.

〉 3.2 Subtraction

Exercise 3.2

Focus

1 Complete each subtraction. Show how you found each answer.

   38 – 5   49 – 7

   =   =

   64 – 7   25 – 8

   =   =

2 Complete each subtraction. Show how you found each answer.

   169 – 6   238 – 4

   =   =

   134 – 8   243 – 7

   =   =

3   Estimate and then complete each subtraction.

184 − 42 = ☐   estimate = 180 − ☐ = ☐

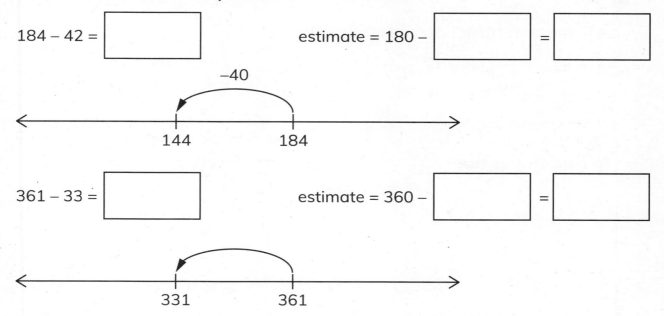

361 − 33 = ☐   estimate = 360 − ☐ = ☐

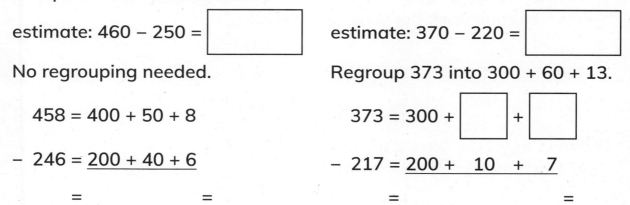

4   Emyr did not have enough time to finish his calculation.
    Complete them both for him.

estimate: 460 − 250 = ☐   estimate: 370 − 220 = ☐

No regrouping needed.   Regroup 373 into 300 + 60 + 13.

  458 = 400 + 50 + 8   373 = 300 + ☐ + ☐

− 246 = 200 + 40 + 6   − 217 = 200 +   10   +   7

    =   =   =   =

Practice

5   Sort these subtractions into the table.

47 – 3   72 – 17   87 – 29   93 – 8

54 – 5   61 – 15   76 – 23   57 – 7

Change a ten for 10 ones to find the answer	No regrouping needed to find the answer

6   The shop has 268 metres of rope. Minh buys 5 metres.
    How much rope does the shop have now?

    _____

    The next day, Loki buys 8 metres of rope.
    How much rope is left in the shop now? _____

7   763 children attend Blue Haven School. 38 children
    are away today. How many children are in school today?

    Estimate and then find the answer. Show your method.

8   There are 362 people on the train. At the first station, 47 people get off and no one gets on. How many people are on the train now?

Estimate and then find the answer. Show your method.

9   763 children attend Blue Haven School.
427 of them are girls.
How many boys are there?

Estimate and then calculate.
Show your method.

10 Estimate and then use an empty number line to help you find the difference between 426 and 483.

_____

Challenge

11 The subtraction machine subtracts 37 from each number in the grid.

Estimate and then complete the answer grid.
How will you find the totals?

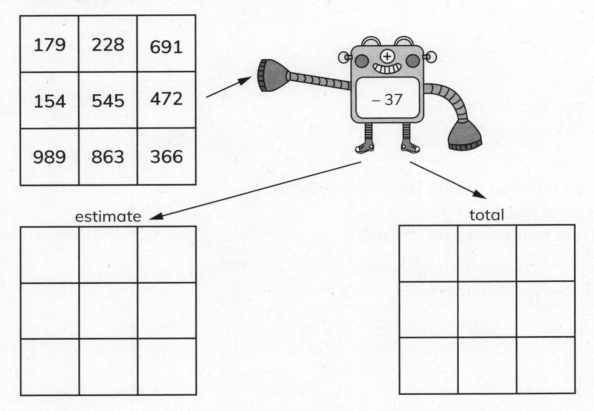

179	228	691
154	545	472
989	863	366

estimate

total

12 Ahliya spilt some ink on the ones digits in her number sentence.

55 ● – 31 ● = 232

What could her calculation have been? Find all the possible answers.

〉 3.3 Money

Exercise 3.3

Focus

buy   change   decimal point   spend

1   Write the missing amounts.

Using dollars and cents	Using a decimal point
$3 and 25c	
$6 and 74c	
$12 and 18c	
	$9.50
	$14.95
	$1.62

2   Use a decimal point to write each amount of money in dollars and cents.

_____

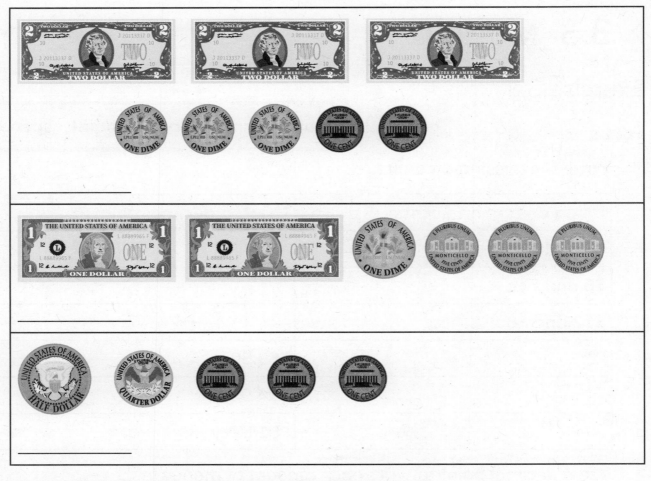

_____

_____

_____

3   Adi has 50c. He buys a pencil and a sharpener.

Eraser 26c   Sharpener 30c   Highlighter 37c

Pencil 18c   Pen 65c   Thick felt pen 45c

How much does he spend? _____

How much change will he have? _____

4   Two bunches of flowers cost $10.
    How much does one bunch of flowers cost?

    Write your number sentence and solve it
    to find the cost of a bunch of flowers.

    You could use a flower or an empty box to
    represent the unknown values in your
    number sentence.

Practice

5   Write the missing amounts.

Using dollars and cents	Using a decimal point
$11 and 9c	
	$65
$0 and 4c	
	$4.01
$0 and 75c	
	$0.99

6   I spent $7 and 25c on a cinema ticket
    and 70c on some popcorn.
    How much did I spend? How much
    change will I get from $10?

Worked example

Two bags of apples cost $7.
How much does one bag of apples cost?

Write your number sentence and solve it to find the
cost of one bag of apples.
Use a picture to represent the unknown value.

+ = $7   I need to find half of $7.

$6 \div 2 = 3$ and $3 + 3 = 6$ I know half of $6 is $3.
Half of $1 = 50c   Half of $1 is 50c.

= $3 + 50c = $3 and 50c

So one bag of apples costs $3   Half of $7 is $3 and 50c.
and 50c.

7   Two plants in pots cost $9.
    How much does one plant in a pot cost?

    Complete your number sentence and solve
    it to find the cost of a plant in a pot.

    You could use a plant or an empty box
    to represent the unknown value in your
    number sentence.

Challenge

8   Sibo writes $7 and 9 cents = $9.7

    What mistake has Sibo made?

    _____

    _____

9   Sarah has $30. She buys a skirt and gets $1 and 1c change.
     How much does the skirt cost?

     Write your number sentence and solve it to find the cost
     of the skirt. You could use a price label or an empty box
     to represent the unknown value in your number sentence.

     _____

     _____

10   Ahmed spends $63 and 25c on new clothes. He has $2 and 75c change.

     How much money did Ahmed have before he bought the clothes?

     _____

4 ▸ 3D shapes

4.1 3D shapes

Exercise 4.1

apex   prism

Worked example

A pyramid has a flat base and flat faces. The faces are triangles.
They join at the top, making an apex.

Draw a ⟨ring⟩ around the shapes that are **not** pyramids.

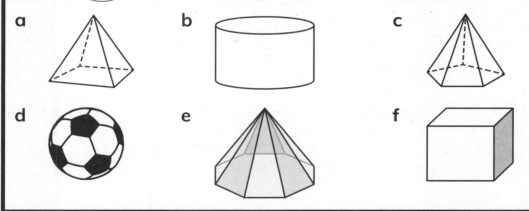

a   b   c

d   e   f

Look at the faces and surfaces of the shapes.

Look for an apex.

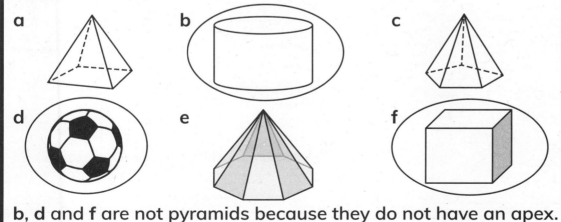

a   b   c

d   e   f

b, d and **f** are not pyramids because they do not have an apex.

Focus

1   A prism has identical ends and flat faces.
The shape at the ends gives the prism a name.

This is a rectangular prism.

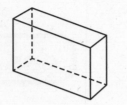

Write the names of each shape. (Ring) the shapes that are prisms.

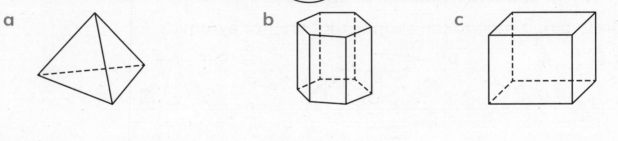

a   b   c

_____   _____   _____

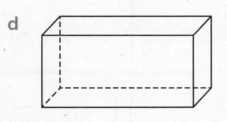   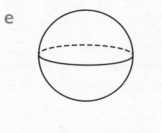   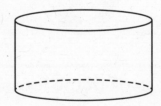

d   e   f

_____   _____   _____

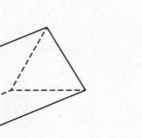   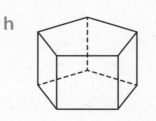   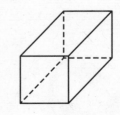

g   h   i

_____   _____   _____

2   For each shape, write its name and the number of vertices
    that it has. Use these words to help you.

square prism   triangle-based pyramid   rectangular prism

square-based pyramid   triangular prism   cylinder

Name _____ Number of vertices ____	Name _____ Number of vertices ____
Name _____ Number of vertices ____	Name _____ Number of vertices ____
Name _____ Number of vertices ____	Name _____ Number of vertices ____

3 a Trace over the dashed lines to show 3D shapes.
Write their names underneath.

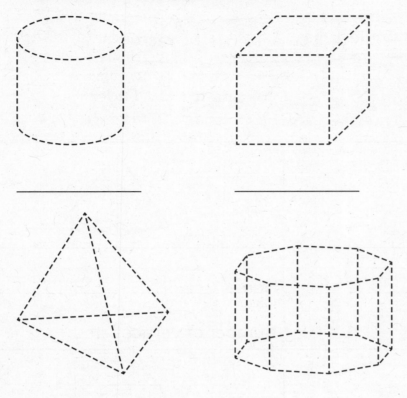

_____   _____

_____   _____

b Sketch two of your own 3D shapes. Make at least one of your
shapes a prism.

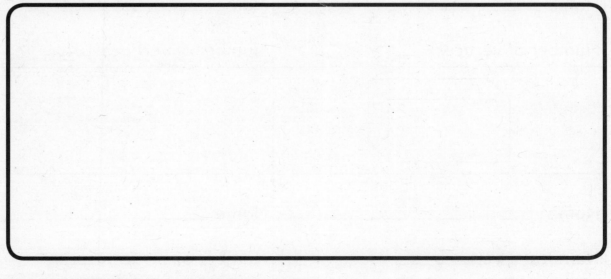

c Tick (✓) the shapes that are prisms.

4   Find or collect 3D shapes in your house.

Match them to these 3D shapes.

Draw what you find.

3D shape	Picture	Your examples
Cube		
Cuboid		
Sphere		
Prism		
Pyramid		
cylinder		

Which shapes from the table can you make using building blocks?

_____

Choose two shapes to make.

Practice

5   For each shape, write whether it is a prism or a pyramid.

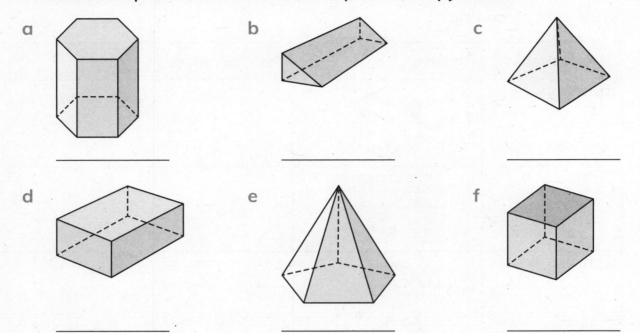

a _____

b _____

c _____

d _____

e _____

f _____

6   Draw and name the 3D shapes.

a   I have six faces and eight vertices.
    I have 12 edges and my faces are all the same shape.

    What am I?

_____

b   I have six faces and eight vertices. I have 12 edges.
    Four of my faces are rectangles, the other two are squares.

    What am I?

    _____

c   If you cut me in half, my end face will remain the same.
    Two of my faces are the same, one is curved.

    What am I?

    _____

d   I have one smooth surface and 0 vertices. I have 0 edges.

    What am I?

    _____

7   Sketch a cube.

Sketch a cuboid.

Challenge

8   Complete the table.

3D shape	Number of faces	Number of edges	Number of vertices
hexagonal prism			
triangular prism			
octagonal prism			
triangular-based pyramid			

9   Look around you. Find two 3D shapes that are cylinders, two that are prisms and two that are neither.

Draw and name them.

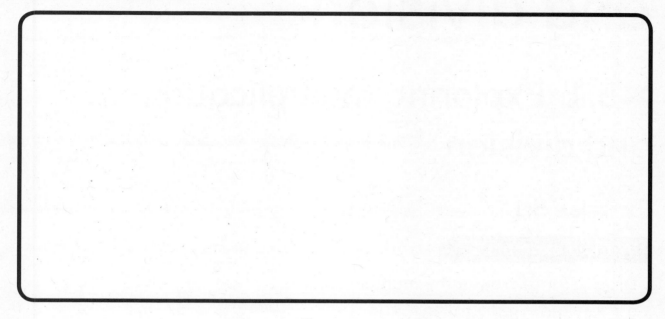

10 Sketch this shape.

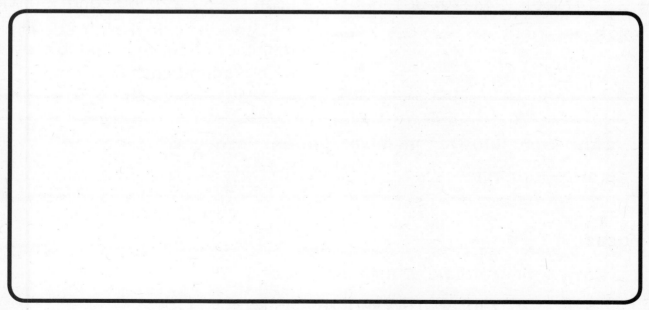

5 ▶ Multiplication and division

> 5.1 Exploring multiplication and division

Exercise 5.1

Worked example 1

Draw a (ring) around the multiples of 10.

23, 147, 60, 194, 220, 381, 600, 425, 276, 390

23, 147, 6<u>0</u>, 194, 22<u>0</u>, 381, 60<u>0</u>, 425, 276, 39<u>0</u>.	Multiples of 10 always have 0 in the ones place.
23, 147, (60), 194, (220), 381, (600), 425, 276, (390).	I can see 60, 220, 600 and 390 with 0 in the ones place. They are all multiples of 10, so I need to draw a ring around each of them.

array   commutative   multiple   pattern   sequence   term
term-to-term rule

Focus

1   Draw a (ring) around all the multiples of 5.

15, 72, 125, 230, 86, 157, 390, 269, 95, 414

2 Mosego sorted the numbers from 20 to 40 into the correct places on the Venn diagram. Finish Mosego's work by putting 35, 36, 37, 38, 39 and 40 into the correct places in the Venn diagram.

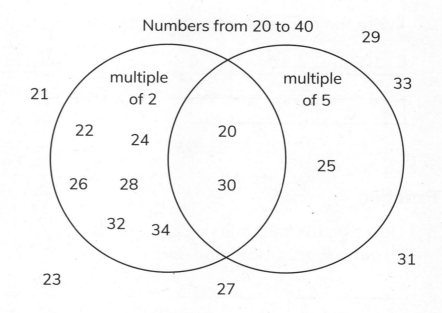

3 Write the fact family for this array.

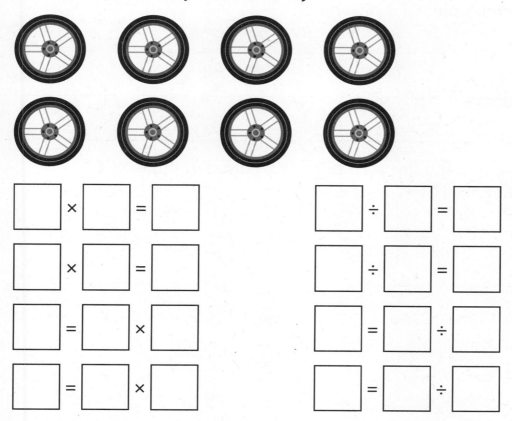

4   Write the multiplying by 10 facts shown here.

100s	10s	1s
		7
	7	0

100s	10s	1s
	1	9
1	9	0

Practice

5   Describe the multiples of 2, 5 and 10.
     Use the words 'odd' and 'even'.

_____

_____

_____

     How are multiples of 2 and 10 the same?
     How are the multiples of 5 different?

_____

_____

_____

6   I am an odd number. I am > 70 but < 80. I am a multiple of 5.
     Which number am I?

_____

7   Which multiplication facts from the 1, 2, 5 and 10 multiplication tables have only four facts in their fact family?

Write the fact family for one of these facts.

8   This machine multiplies numbers by 10. Complete the grid to record the numbers after they come out of the machine.

74	9	56
6	82	29
17	38	5
3	94	61

Challenge

9   I am an even number. I am > 374 but < 386.
I am a multiple of 2, 5 and 10. Which number am I?

10

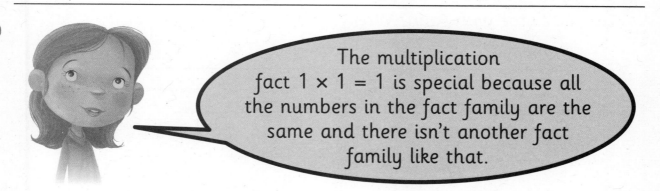

The multiplication fact 1 × 1 = 1 is special because all the numbers in the fact family are the same and there isn't another fact family like that.

Find a different special multiplication fact from the
1, 2, 5, 10 fact families. Explain why it is special.

_____

_____

_____

11 Binh has ten 65 cm lengths of timber.
What is the total length of timber that Binh has?

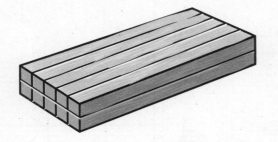

_____

 12

$0 \times 10 = 10$, because
multiplying by 10 makes any number
ten times larger.

Do you agree with Arun? Why?

_____

_____

_____

> 5.2 Connecting 2 ×, 4 × and 8 ×

Exercise 5.2

Focus

1   Which multiplication fact is represented below?

 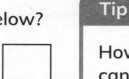

> **Tip**
>
> How many fours can you see?

2   Write the multiplication table for 4, up to 4 × 10 = 40.

3   Colour all the multiples of 8.

1	2	3	4	5	6	7	8	9	10
11	12	13	14	15	16	17	18	19	20
21	22	23	24	25	26	27	28	29	30
31	32	33	34	35	36	37	38	39	40
41	42	43	44	45	46	47	48	49	50

4   There are six spiders on a plant. Write and solve
the multiplication fact to find out how
many spiders' legs are on the plant.

Worked example 2

The term-to-term rule is 'add 4'.

Start at 2. What are the next five numbers in the sequence?

2, ☐, ☐, ☐, ☐, ☐

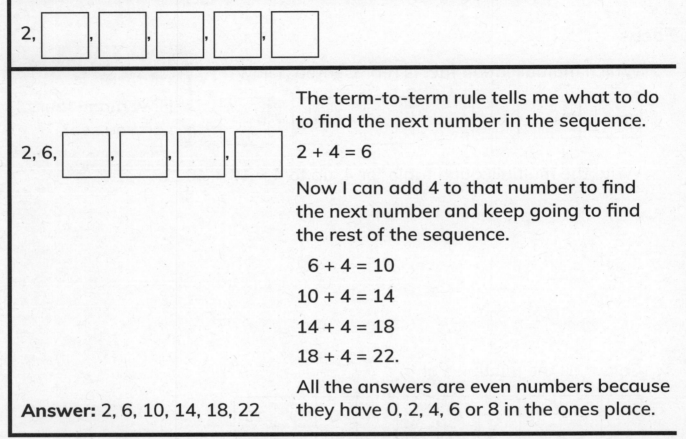

2, 6, ☐, ☐, ☐, ☐

The term-to-term rule tells me what to do to find the next number in the sequence.

$2 + 4 = 6$

Now I can add 4 to that number to find the next number and keep going to find the rest of the sequence.

$6 + 4 = 10$

$10 + 4 = 14$

$14 + 4 = 18$

$18 + 4 = 22.$

All the answers are even numbers because they have 0, 2, 4, 6 or 8 in the ones place.

Answer: 2, 6, 10, 14, 18, 22

5   The term-to-term rule is 'add 4'.

Start at 3. What are the next five numbers in the sequence?

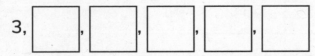

3, ☐, ☐, ☐, ☐, ☐

Describe the numbers you have written using words such as odd and even.

Practice

6   What is the third multiple of 4? ☐

    What is the 7th multiple of 4? ☐

7   What are the next five multiples of 4?

    40, ☐ , ☐ , ☐ , ☐ , ☐

8   Describe the pattern of the multiples of 4.

    _____

    _____

9   What is the fifth multiple of 8? ☐

    What is the 9th multiple of 8? ☐

10 Write the missing multiplication facts.

	double →	4 × 4 = 16	double →	
2 × 2 = 4	double →		double →	
	← halve		← halve	8 × 8 = 64
2 × 7 = 14	← halve		← halve	

> **Tip**
>
> Remember to change the group size and the product in the same way to find the new multiplication table fact. The number of groups doesn't change.

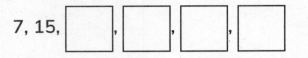

11 What is the term-to-term rule in the sequence below?
Find the missing numbers.

7, 15, ☐ , ☐ , ☐ , ☐

The term-to-term rule is _____ .

Describe the numbers you have written using words such as
odd and even.

_____

Challenge

12 Complete the multiplication grid.

×	2	4	8
3			
5	10	20	
6			
9			

13 A pear costs 8c.
Write the multiplication fact that
tells you the cost of seven pears.

_____

14 A white T-shirt costs $4.
Write the multiplication fact that tells you the cost of 8 T-shirts.

_____

15 Tara's father bought six pieces of timber, each measuring 4 metres long. What is the total length of timber that Tara's father bought?

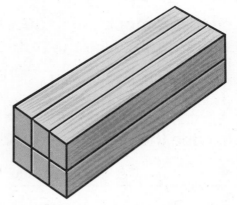

_____

16 Choose a term-to-term rule, a start number and how many terms to record. Write your sequence.

> 5.3 Connecting 3 ×, 6 × and 9 ×

Exercise 5.3

Focus

counting stick

1 Use the number line to help you find the multiples of 3.

3, ☐ , ☐ , ☐ , ☐ , ☐ , ☐ , ☐ , ☐ , 30

Describe the numbers you have written using words such as odd and even.

_____

2   Use the number line in question 1 to help you find the
    multiples of 6. Use the pattern to help you continue to 60.

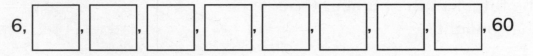

6, ☐, ☐, ☐, ☐, ☐, ☐, ☐, ☐, 60

Describe the numbers you have written using words such as odd and even.

_____

3   Write the missing multiplication facts.

3 × 2 = 6	double →	
3 × 6 = 18	double →	
	← halve	6 × 4 = 24
	← halve	6 × 1 = 6

Tip

Remember to change the group size and the product in the same way to find the new multiplication table fact. The number of groups doesn't change.

4   Multiply together the numbers in the bricks
    next to each other to find the number for the
    brick above.

a

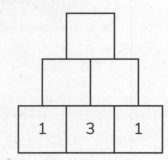

b

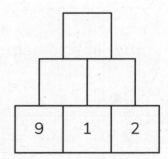

5   The term-to-term rule is add 9.

Start at 8 and write the next five numbers in your sequence.

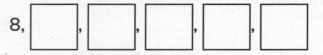

8, ☐, ☐, ☐, ☐

Describe the numbers you have written using words such as odd and even.

_____

Practice

6   Multiply together the numbers in the bricks next to each
    other to find the number for the brick above.

a
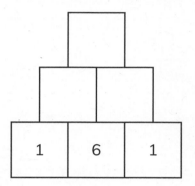

b
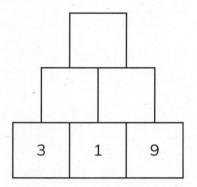

7   Ruby the red kangaroo jumps 9 metres in
    each jump. How far does she travel with
    seven jumps? Write the multiplication fact
    that helps you to find out.

    _____

8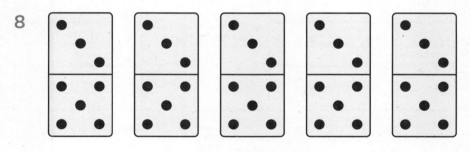

    $8 × 5 = \underline{5 × 5} + \underline{3 × 5} = 25 + 15 = 40$

    Draw a picture on the next page to show how you can add the
    multiplication tables for 5 and 4 together to find $9 × 6$.

9 Write the missing multiplication facts.

			+ 3× and 6×	
	double →	6 × 3 = 18		
3 × 10 = 30	double →			
	← halve	6 × 9 = 54	together →	
3 × 0 = 0	← halve			

Tip

Add groups of 3 and groups of 6 together to get groups of 9.

$$3 \times 3 = 9$$
$$+ 6 \times 3 = 18$$
$$\overline{9 \times 3 = 27}$$

Challenge

10 102, 108, 114 and 120 are multiples of 3 and 6.
Which multiples of 3 and 6 are they?

102 _____

108 _____

114 _____

120 _____

11 The term-to-term rule is – 9.

Start at 100. What are the next five numbers in the sequence?

100, ☐ , ☐ , ☐ , ☐ , ☐

Is 1 part of this sequence? How do you know?

_____

12 Zara finds it hard to remember the multiplication
table for 9. She says that she can use the
multiplication table for 10, then subtract 1
from the product for each 9.

Do you agree? Why?

_____

_____

_____

6 Measurement, area and perimeter

> 6.1 Measurement

Exercise 6.1

Focus

1 a   Write something that you can measure using each unit of length.

Remember that 1 kilometre = 1000 metres
1 metre = 100 centimetres

Unit of length	What could you measure?
Kilometres (km)	
Metres (m)	
Centimetres (cm)	

b   What could have these measurements? Make your answers different from the ones above.

1 kilometre _____

1 metre _____

1 centimetre _____

2 Use a ruler.

Estimate and then measure each of these lines in centimetres.

a _____

estimate: _____   measure: _____

b _____

estimate: _____   measure: _____

c _____

estimate: _____   measure: _____

d Draw lines of lengths 2 cm, 5 cm and 7 cm. Label them.

3 Draw a ⟨ring⟩ around the correct answers.

a How many metres are in half a kilometre?

$\frac{1}{2}$ kilometre =   1000 m   500 m   10 m

b How many metres in $\frac{1}{4}$ kilometre?

$\frac{1}{4}$ km =   25 m   250 m   750 m

c   How many centimetres in 1 metre?

1 m =   10 cm   100 cm   1000 cm

d   How many metres in $\frac{3}{4}$ kilometre?

$\frac{3}{4}$ km =   75 m   450 m   750 m

Show how you worked out the answer to part **d**.

4   Find the length of the objects, to the nearest centimetre.

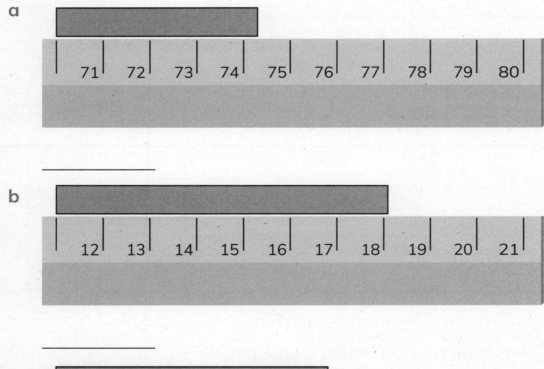

a

b

c

Practice

5   a   Estimate the distance from your bedroom to the kitchen.

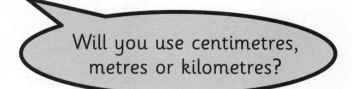

Will you use centimetres, metres or kilometres?

estimate: _____

How could you find out what the length is?

_____

b   Estimate the distance from your house to the nearest shop.

Use either centimetres, metres or kilometres. Explain your choice.

_____

_____

6   Complete the sentence.
Round the answer to the nearest centimetre.

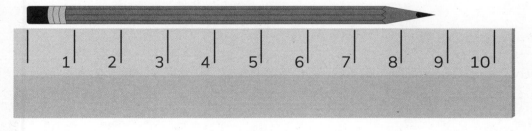

The length of the pencil is about ____ cm.

7 **a** Estimate then measure the height of each picture.

estimate: _____

measure: _____

estimate: _____

measure: _____

b Draw and measure a person shorter than Arun.

8 Draw a (ring) around the correct answers.

a How many centimetres are in three and a half metres?

300 cm   350 cm   35 cm

b How many centimetres are in five and a quarter metres?

550 cm   575 cm   525 cm   500 cm

c 500 cm = _____ m

d 250 cm = _____ m

e Which is more: $\frac{3}{4}$ m or 700 cm?

Challenge

9 a Find the lengths of the key and paper clip, to the nearest centimetre.

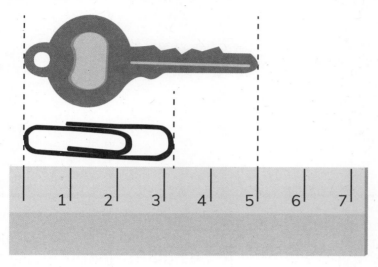

Length of key: _____ cm   Length of paper clip: _____ cm

b Use this ruler to measure four things in your house.

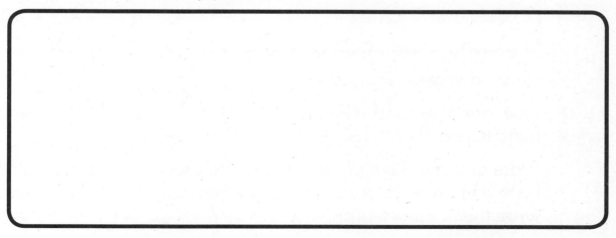

Round the measurements to the nearest centimetre.

Draw and label what you have found.

10 a Collect four objects that you estimate to be 20 cm long.

Sketch them and then measure them.

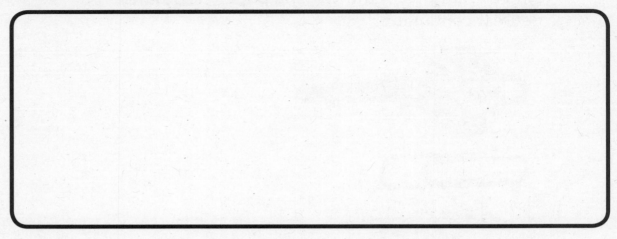

How close were your estimates? _____

b Find four objects that you estimate to be half the length of the others.

Sketch them and then measure them.

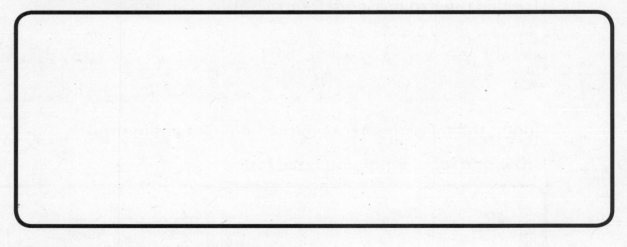

How close were your estimates? _____

11 a Find four objects that you estimate to be between 1 metre and 2 metres long.

Write or draw them in the table. Write their estimated length. If you have a metre stick or tape measure, you can measure them and write their actual length.

Object	Estimated length	Actual length

b   Is there a place that you would like to visit? Estimate whether it is more or less than a kilometre from your house.

_____

How could you find out the actual distance?

_____

12 Complete the number sentences.

a $\frac{3}{4}$ m = _____ cm

b 10 m = _____ cm

c 250 m = _____ km

d 750 m = _____ km

e Write three number sentences of your own.

_____

_____

_____

> 6.2 2D shapes and perimeter

Exercise 6.2

Focus

1 Inside each grid, use the dots to draw a four-sided shape.

Write 'regular' or 'irregular' below each shape.

| centi |
| irregular shape |
| kilo |
| perimeter |
| regular shape |

a

b

_____

_____

c   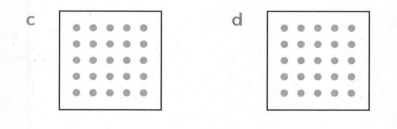   d

_____   _____

2   a   What is the perimeter of this square?

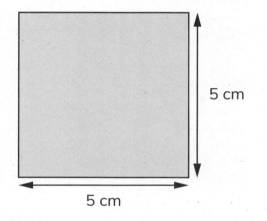

5 cm

5 cm

_____

b   Draw a square with a perimeter of 16 cm. Use your ruler.

How long is each side? _____

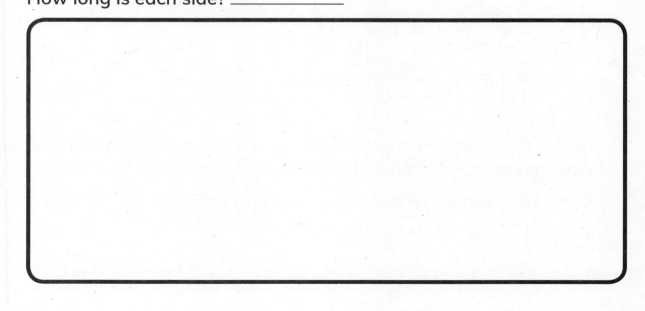

c   What is the perimeter of this regular triangle? _____

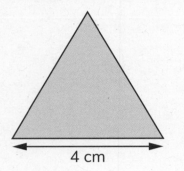

4 cm

3   a   Estimate the length of each side. Use a ruler
        to measure.

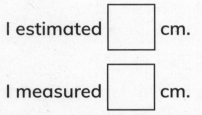

I estimated ⬚ cm.

I measured ⬚ cm.

b   How many centimetres was your estimate
    away from the measurement?

 cm

c   Work out the perimeter of the shape.

The perimeter is ⬚ cm.

Show how you worked that out.

4   Find these shapes in your home or garden. If you can't find any, choose a
    way to make them. You can use stones, twigs or any other materials.

Draw each shape. Write at least two properties for each shape.

The first one is done for you.

Shape	Your drawing	Properties
Square		4 vertices 4 straight sides All the sides are the same length
Rectangle		
Triangle		
Pentagon		
Hexagon		

Choose one of your drawings. Find the perimeter.

_____

Practice

5 Use the dots to draw three different regular shapes and three irregular shapes.

Label them.

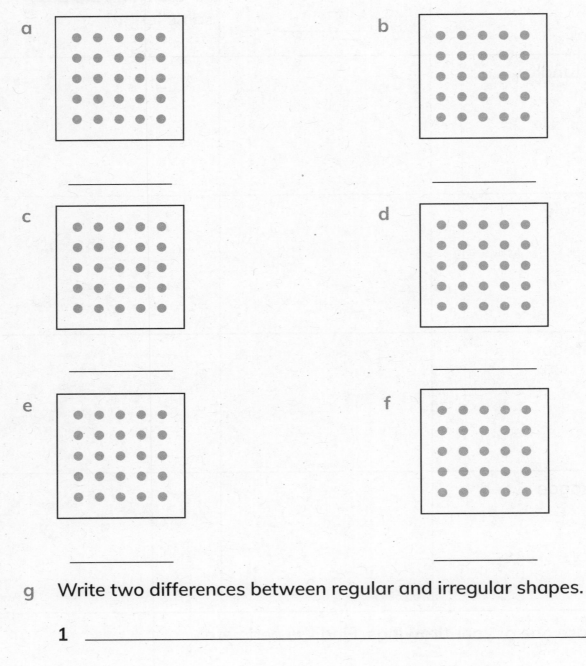

a

b

c

d

e

f

g Write two differences between regular and irregular shapes.

1 _____

2 _____

6 a   Measure this square.

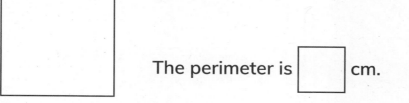

The perimeter is [ ] cm.

b   Halve the length of its sides and draw it here.

The perimeter is [ ] cm.

c   Double the length of its sides and draw it here.

The perimeter is [ ] cm.

7 **a** Estimate the lengths of these sides.

estimate: _____

measure: _____

b My estimate was _____ away from the measured length.

c What is the perimeter of the square? _____
Show how you worked that out.

Challenge

8 **a** Use the dots to draw three squares that each have sides the same length but look different.

b Use the dots to draw three triangles with sides the same length but look different.

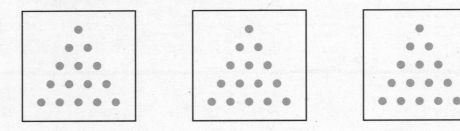

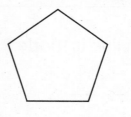

9   a   This pentagon has sides of 16 metres.

What is its perimeter? _____
Show how you worked out the answer.

b   Use a ruler to draw a rectangle. Choose the length of it sides.
Calculate the perimeter.

10 a   Estimate the length of these sides, then use a ruler
to measure them.

estimate: _____

measure: _____

b   Calculate the perimeter of the octagon.

_____

c   If each line is made 2 cm longer, what will be the perimeter?

> 6.3 Introducing area

Exercise 6.3

area   square units

> **Worked example**

This shape is drawn on a grid made up of nine whole squares.
How many whole squares are inside the shape?

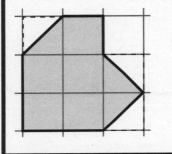

This shape has been made with six and a half squares:
five whole squares and three half squares.

Focus

1   How many whole squares are inside each shape?

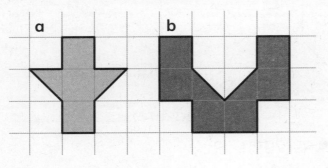

2 Complete the triangle.

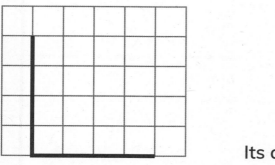

Its area is ☐ square units.

3 Find the areas and perimeters of these shapes using square units.

Shape	Area	Perimeter
a		
b		
c		
d		

e What is the area and perimeter of the next shape in the series?

Draw it. _____

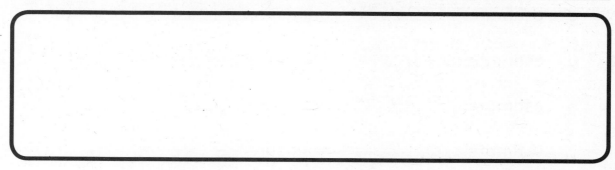

f   What do you notice about the numbers that you have written for the area and the perimeter?

_____

_____

Practice

4   Estimate and calculate the area of these shapes using square units.

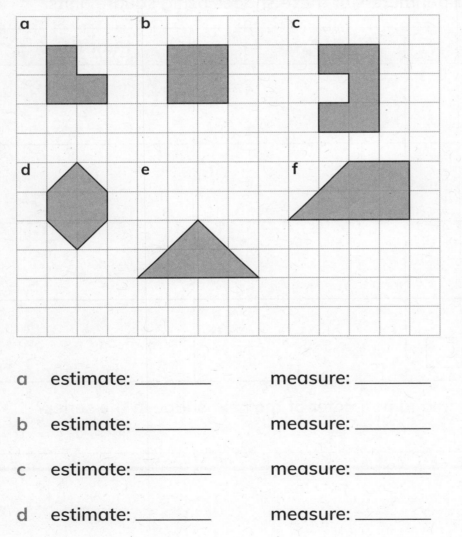

a   estimate: _____   measure: _____

b   estimate: _____   measure: _____

c   estimate: _____   measure: _____

d   estimate: _____   measure: _____

e   estimate: _____   measure: _____

f   estimate: _____   measure: _____

5   Draw lines to join the pairs of shapes that have the same area.

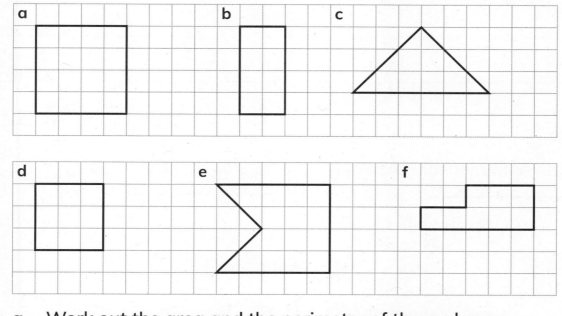

6   a   Work out the area and the perimeter of these shapes
       using square units.

Square	Area	Perimeter
□		
⊞		
⊞		
⊞		

   b   Can you predict the area and the perimeter of the next
       shape in the series?

_____

c   What do you notice about the area and the perimeter of 16 squares?

_____

_____

Challenge

7   Estimate then measure the length of the sides of these shapes.

a

b

estimate: _____

estimate: _____

measure: _____

measure: _____

c

d

estimate: _____

estimate: _____

measure: _____

measure: _____

e   Which shape has the largest area? _____

8   a   Draw a rectangle with an area of 12 square units.

b   Draw any shape with an area of 13 and a half square units.

9 Imagine a square that has an area of 25 square units.

a How long are each of its sides?

_____

b How long is the perimeter? Show your working.

_____

7 ▶ Fractions of shapes

> 7.1 Fractions and equivalence of shapes

Exercise 7.1

> denominator
> equal
> equivalent
> fifths
> numerator
> tenths
> thirds

Worked example 1

This rectangle has four equal parts.

It is divided into quarters. One part is called one-quarter.

a   Colour three-quarters.

b   How many quarters are not coloured?

a

b   There is one-quarter not coloured.

Count the empty squares to find the number that are not coloured.

Focus

1 For each shape, shade the fraction shown below it.

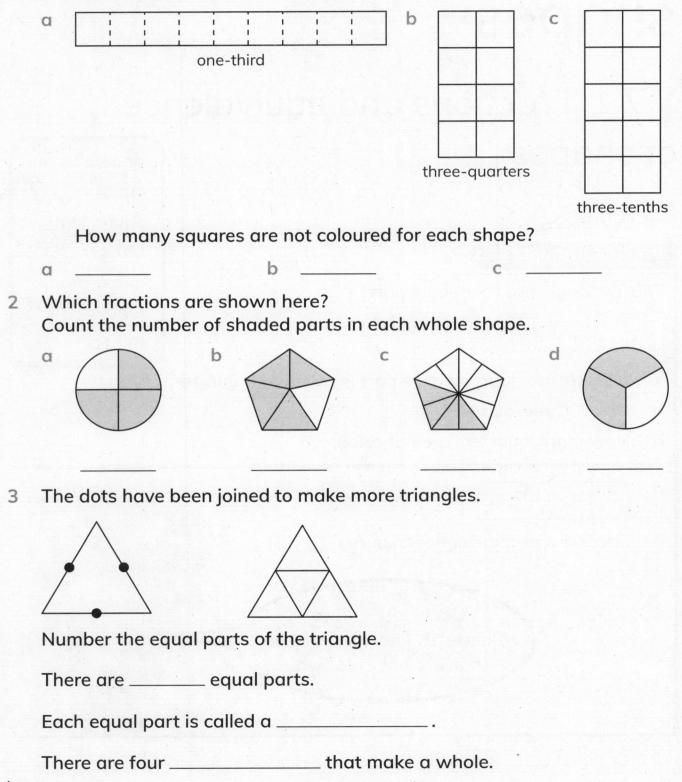

a

one-third

b

three-quarters

c

three-tenths

How many squares are not coloured for each shape?

a _____   b _____   c _____

2 Which fractions are shown here?
Count the number of shaded parts in each whole shape.

a   b   c   d

_____   _____   _____   _____

3 The dots have been joined to make more triangles.

Number the equal parts of the triangle.

There are _____ equal parts.

Each equal part is called a _____ .

There are four _____ that make a whole.

Practice

4   Divide each of these shapes into two identical and equal parts.

Count the number of small squares in each shape.

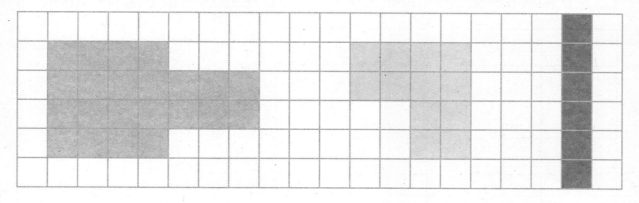

_____   _____   _____

Draw shapes that can be divided into three equal parts.

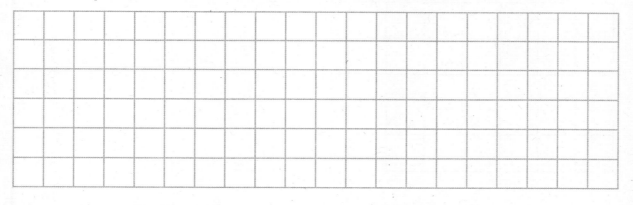

Draw shapes that can be divided into ten equal parts.

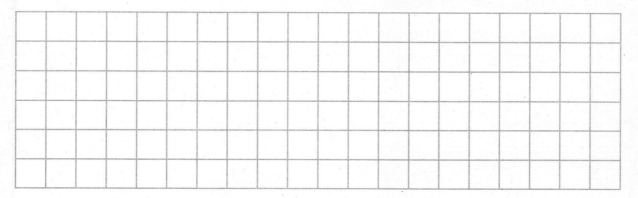

5   Colour two different ways to show one-third of this rectangle.

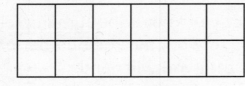 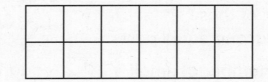

Colour two different ways to show three-quarters of this rectangle.

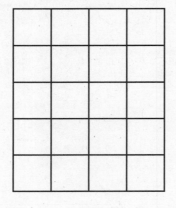 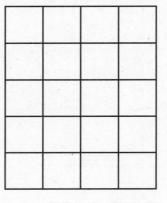

Colour two different ways to show four-tenths in this rectangle.

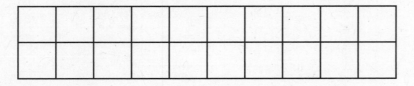

Tip

Work out what one-tenth is first.

6   Draw equivalent fractions to match the ones on the left.
    Write each fraction. Use fifths and tenths.

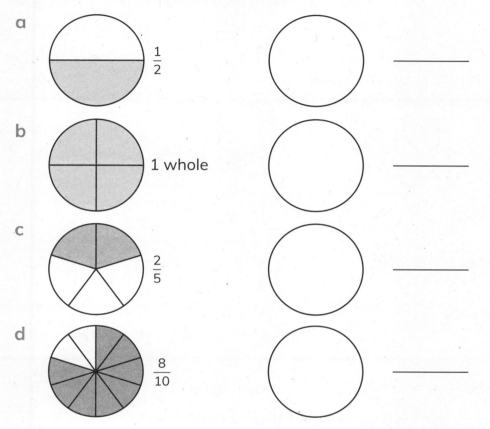

a $\frac{1}{2}$ _____

b   1 whole   _____

c $\frac{2}{5}$ _____

d $\frac{8}{10}$ _____

Challenge

7   Write the fractions.

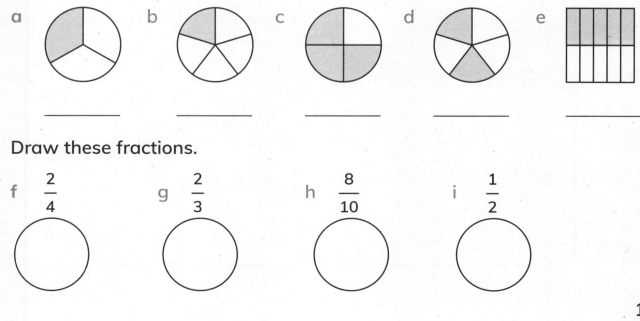

a   b   c   d   e

_____   _____   _____   _____   _____

Draw these fractions.

f $\frac{2}{4}$ g $\frac{2}{3}$ h $\frac{8}{10}$ i $\frac{1}{2}$

8   This is a third of a shape.

    a   Draw two different whole shapes.

    b   Now imagine it is one fifth of a whole shape.

       Draw two different whole shapes that it could be.

9 Put a tick (✓) in the box if the fractions are equivalent.

Put a cross in the box if they are not equivalent.

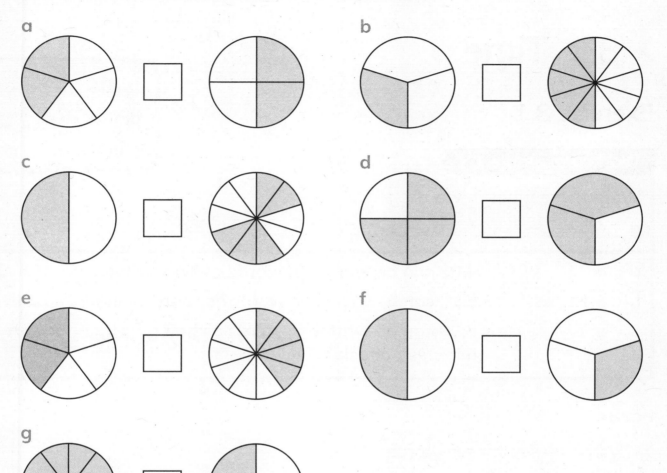

8 ► Time

> 8.1 Time

Exercise 8.1

analogue clock
digital clock
minute

Worked example 1 ►

Write these times in words.

a 4:02   b 5:12   c 8:30

---

a	4:02	4:02 can be written in words as two minutes past four.
b	5:12	5:12 can be written in words as twelve minutes past five.
c	8:30	8:30 can be written in words as half past eight or thirty minutes past eight.

Focus

1 Write these times in words.

a 6:01

_____

b 3:30

_____

c 12:14

_____

d 8:45

_____

2 Write these times in digital form.

a half past eight [__ : __]

b thirty-four minutes past two [__ : __]

c four o'clock [__ : __]

d forty-two minutes past six [__ : __]

3 Fill in the empty digital clocks.

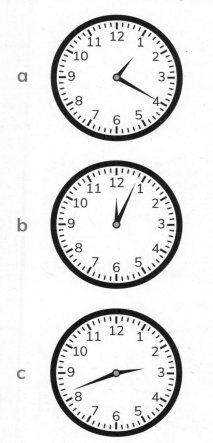

a [__ : __]

b [__ : __]

c [__ : __]

Practice

4   Draw the hands on the clocks to show the correct time.

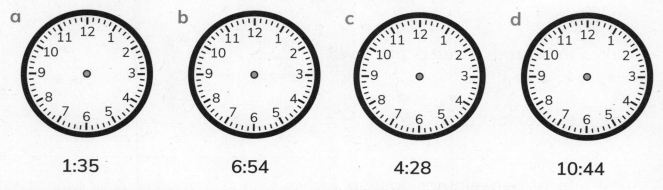

a   b   c   d

1:35   6:54   4:28   10:44

5   Write three digital times that come between the times shown.

07:48   09:12

:   :   :

6   Draw the hands on the analogue clock to match the digital time.

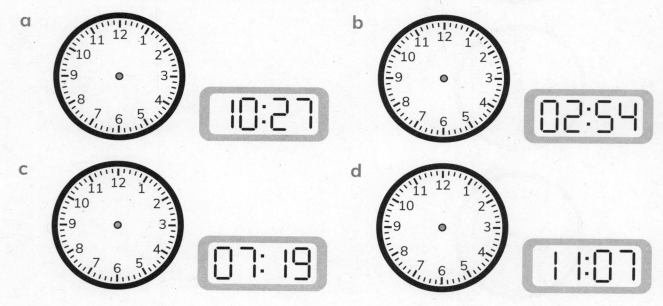

a   b

10:27   02:54

c   d

07:19   11:07

Challenge

7 Complete these sentences.

a 3:45 is the same as quarter to _____

b A quarter to two can be written as _____

c A quarter to eleven can be written as _____

d 10:15 can be written as _____

e 1:45 is the same as quarter to _____

8 Dembe looks at her digital watch and sees that each number is one higher than the number to its left.

Find three different times that she might see.

Write the times alongside, using words for analogue times.

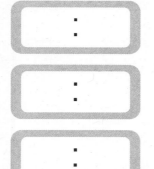

_____

_____

_____

9 Write any time that comes between the two times shown.

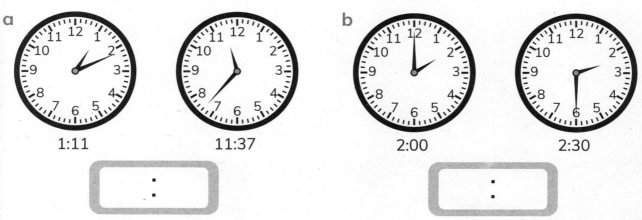

a
1:11   11:37

b
2:00   2:30

c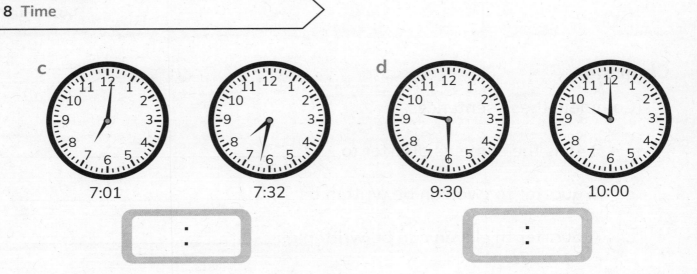

7:01   7:32   9:30   10:00

10 a What time do you get up in the morning? Draw hands on the analogue clock and write the numbers on the digital clock.

b What time do you go to bed in the evening? Draw hands on the analogue clock and write the numbers on the digital clock.

9 More addition and subtraction

> 9.1 Addition: regrouping tens and reordering

Exercise 9.1

associative   column addition   commutative

Focus

1   Estimate the total. Find the total and represent it in the place value grid. Complete the number sentence.

100s	10s	1s
	●● ●●	○○ ○○
	●●● ●●● ●●●	○ ○ ○ ○ ○

estimate: _____

100s	10s	1s

☐ + ☐ = ☐

2   Estimate and then solve these 2-digit number additions.
    Show your method.

    a   estimate: b   estimate:

        53 + 76   65 + 54

        =   =

    c   estimate: d   estimate:

        46 + 81   66 + 42

3   Estimate and then solve these additions. Show your method.

    a   estimate: b   estimate:

        129 + 60   187 + 50

        =   =

    c   estimate: d   estimate:

        164 + 71   245 + 172

        =   =

4 Write one thousand in numbers.
How many hundreds are there in one thousand?

_____

_____

5 Add these single-digit numbers together in two different ways.
Is there a complement of 10 that you can use to help you?

> **Tip**
>
> Reorder the numbers to help you add. Remember, addition is commutative and associative!

Practice

6 Sort these additions into the table.

25 + 57	75 + 63	34 + 52	28 + 61
54 + 82	96 + 21	34 + 38	69 + 27
43 + 55	36 + 46	46 + 31	67 + 52

No regrouping	Regrouping ones	Regrouping tens

7 How do you know if you need to regroup ones when adding?

_____

_____

8   Tick (✓) the true statements.

When I add a 3-digit number and some tens:

a   the ones digit does not change ☐

b   the tens digit always changes ☐

c   the hundreds digit always changes ☐

9   Estimate and then solve these additions. Show your method.

a   estimate:

135 + 73

=

b   estimate:

245 + 272

=

c   estimate:

571 + 243

=

d   estimate:

352 + 153

=

10 Sofia says that the only new number word that she learned in Stage 3 was thousand. Is she correct? Explain why.

_____

_____

11 Nawaf adds three different single-digit numbers. His total is 18.

Find three different sets of three numbers with a total of 18.
Which complements of 10 did you use?

12 Estimate and then add 375, 321 and 283. Show your method.

estimate:

Challenge

13 a   Oditi adds a 3-digit number and some tens. Her total is 364.
         What could her numbers be?

    b   Wen finds six possible solutions.
         Can you find more than six solutions?

14 Add the single-digit numbers in each balloon together.
    Show your method.

> **Tip**
>
> Remember, addition
> is commutative and
> associative!

Compare your method with your partner's method.
How are they the same? How are they different?

15   Here are Afua's column additions.

```
    154              227
    151              213
  + 243            + 334
  ─────            ─────
      8               14
    140               60
  + 400            + 700
  ─────            ─────
    548              774
  ─────            ─────
```

Why do you think that Afua recorded her 3-digit numbers
in the order shown?

_____

_____

_____

> 9.2 Subtraction: regrouping tens

Exercise 9.2

Focus

1   Estimate the answer.
    Find and represent your answer in the place value grid. Complete the number sentence.

    estimate:

    158 – 73 =

exchange

regroup

trial and improvement

unknown

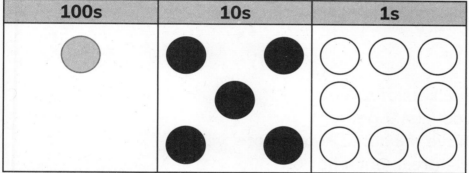

100s	10s	1s

☐ − ☐ = ☐

2   Estimate and then solve these subtractions. Show your method.

   a   estimate: b   estimate:

      178 – 53   267 – 64

      =   =

   c   estimate: d   estimate:

      154 – 72   236 – 84

      =   =

3   Mum buys two packets of sweets.
   There are 42 sweets all together.
   If both packets have the same number of sweets,
   how many sweets are in each packet?
   Use trial and improvement to help you find your answer.

   The unknown value is represented by a sweet.

      + = 42   So   =

Practice

4 Sort these subtractions into the table.

188 – 54	337 – 119	345 – 213	247 – 163
269 – 182	276 – 163	437 – 264	257 – 125
143 – 28	736 – 283	296 – 158	172 – 127

No regrouping	Regrouping ones	Regrouping tens

5 How do you know if you need to regroup tens when subtracting?

_____

_____

6 Estimate and then solve the subtractions that you sorted
into the regrouping tens part of the table in question 4.
Show your method.

Share and discuss your methods with your partner.

7   Here is Danh's calculation of 419 − 187.
    What mistakes has Danh made?

    estimate: 410 − 180 = 230

       419 = 400 + 10 + 9

    − 187 = <u>100 + 80 + 7</u>

           300 + 70 + 2 = 372

    Check: 372 + 187 = 559

    _____

    _____

    _____

    _____

8   A newspaper shop has 364 newspapers delivered
    early in the morning. By lunchtime there are only 83 left.
    How many newspapers have been sold? The unknown
    value is represented by a newspaper.
    Use trial and improvement to help you find out.

    364 − [newspaper] = 83   So [newspaper] = ☐

Challenge

9   When you subtract 90 from a 3-digit number, you will
    need to exchange 1 hundred for 10 tens.
    Is this always true, sometimes true, or never true?
    Explain your answer.

    _____

    _____

10 There are 764 children in the school.
   392 of them are girls.
   How many boys are there?

   Write your number sentence and show your method.
   Remember to estimate before you calculate.

11 Kwanza buys two identical footballs.
   Kwanza pays $38 for the footballs.
   What is the price of each football? The unknown
   price of each football is represented by a football.
   Use trial and improvement to help you find out.

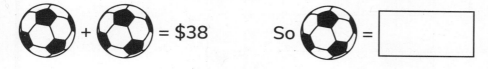

   Explain to your partner what you did to find your answer.

12 Aarvi and her family are travelling 354 kilometres to visit
   her grandparents.
   When the family stops for lunch, they have 171 kilometres to go.
   How far have they travelled when they stop for lunch?
   The unknown value is represented by a car.
   Use trial and improvement to help you find out.

   354 – 🚗 = 171   So 🚗 = ☐

> 9.3 Complements

Exercise 9.3

blank   complement

Focus

1   Which complements of 100 are shown on the blank 100 squares?
    Write the matching number sentences.

a

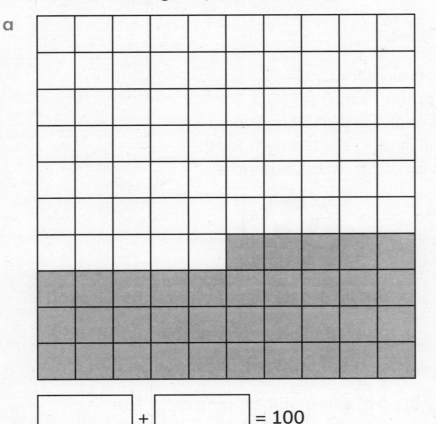

☐ + ☐ = 100

b

$\boxed{}$ + $\boxed{}$ = 100

2   What are the six complements of 1000, using multiples of 100?

Practice

3   Find the complement of 100 for each number.
    Write your answer in the matching square of the grid.

19	82	93
46	78	37
3	51	64

→ complement
of 100

4 Use the complements that you found in question 3 to
   write nine number sentences that have a total of 100.

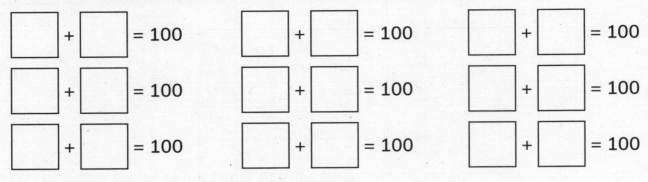

5 Find all the pairs of numbers with 5 tens that are
   complements of 1000.

6 Here are Ibrahim's estimates. Complete the calculations
   for him. Remember to calculate mentally to find the estimates.

a   410 + 240 = ⬚   b   720 + 180 = ⬚

c   940 − 340 = ⬚   d   530 − 270 = ⬚

Challenge

7 Use complements of 100 to help you solve these problems.

   a   There are 100 books on the bookshelf.
       23 are borrowed.
       How many books are left on the shelf?

b   Liling has 100 marbles.
    She lost 17 of them.
    How many marbles does she have left?

c   Luiz has $100.
    He spends $38.
    How much money does he have left?

d   43 cm was cut off a 1 metre length of string.
    How long is the remaining piece?

e   There are 100 pencils in a pack.
    32 children are given a new pencil.
    How many pencils are left?

8   Complete the complements of 100 cross-number puzzle. The answer to each clue is the complement for 100 for that number.

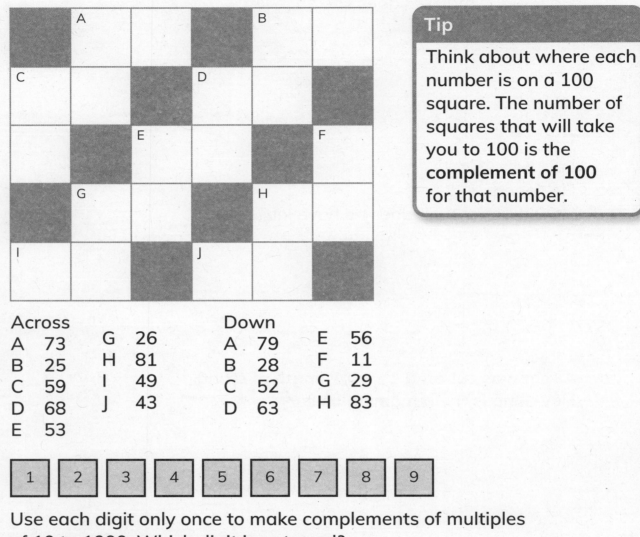

Tip

Think about where each number is on a 100 square. The number of squares that will take you to 100 is the **complement of 100** for that number.

Across
A   73   G   26
B   25   H   81
C   59   I   49
D   68   J   43
E   53

Down
A   79   E   56
B   28   F   11
C   52   G   29
D   63   H   83

9

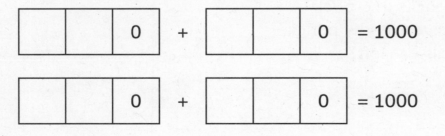

Use each digit only once to make complements of multiples of 10 to 1000. Which digit is not used?

$$\boxed{\ \ 0} + \boxed{\ \ 0} = 1000$$

$$\boxed{\ \ 0} + \boxed{\ \ 0} = 1000$$

The unused digit is _____.

Compare your solution with your partner's.
If they are different, are they both correct?

10 Here are Tuyen's estimates. Complete the calculations for him. Remember to calculate mentally to find the answers.

a   170 + 390 =

b   420 − 280 =

c   960 − 570 =

d   430 + 490 =

e   840 − 490 =

f   750 − 670 =

11 I am a 3-digit complement of a multiple of 10 less than 1000.

My digits add up to 16.

The digits of the 3-digit number that my complement and I add to has digits that total to 17.

What number could I be?
What number could my 3-digit multiple of 10 complement be?

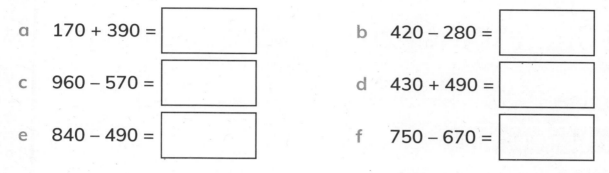

10 ▶ Graphs

> 10.1 Pictograms and bar charts

Exercise 10.1

Worked example 1

On which day did the bookshop sell most books?

Books sold at the bookshop

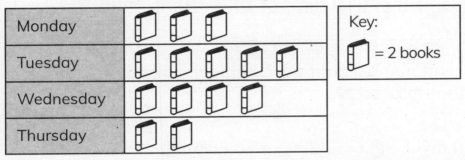

Monday	📖 📖 📖
Tuesday	📖 📖 📖 📖 📖
Wednesday	📖 📖 📖 📖
Thursday	📖 📖

Key:

📖 = 2 books

axes

axis

discrete data

represent

The bookshop sold most books on Tuesday.

The key shows that each book represents two books, so ten books were sold on Tuesday.

Focus

1   Look at this pictogram from a phone shop.

Title:

Tuesday	
Wednesday	
Thursday	
Friday	

a   Write the title for the pictogram

b   How many phones were sold on Friday? _____

c   How many phones were sold on Wednesday? _____

d   How many phones were sold all together? _____

e   On which day were the most number of phones sold? _____

f   On which day were the least number of phones sold? _____

g   Make your own phone pictogram.
    Ask two questions about it. Complete the key.

Key

=

1   _____

2   _____

2 Correct the data on the bar chart.

Six people like cricket.

Three people like golf.

Five people like tennis.

Seven people like football.

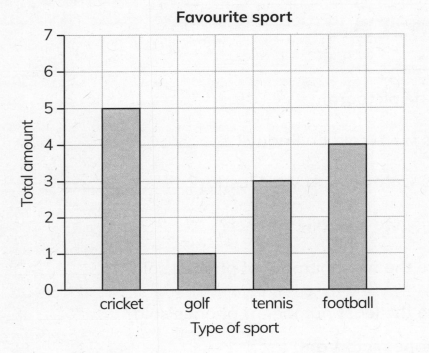

Favourite sport

a How many people were asked all together? _____

b Which sport is liked the most?

_____

c Which sport is liked the least?

_____

d Write the sports in order, starting with the least liked.

_____

_____

3   This pictogram shows how many families visited the park
    on different days of the week.

Visits to the park

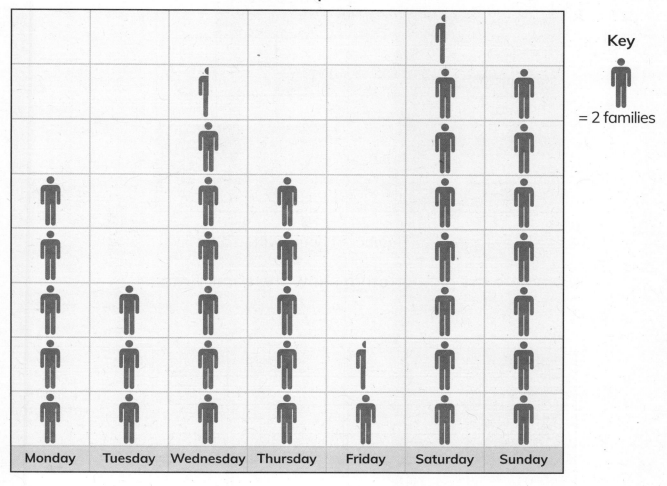

Key = 2 families

a   Which day did most families visit the park? _____

b   Which day did the fewest families visit the park? _____

c   How many families went on Tuesday? _____

d   How many families went on Wednesday? _____

e   Write a question of your own and give the answer.

    _____

    _____

4 This bar chart shows the number of hours of cloud last week. Each space is one hour.

Amount of cloud each day

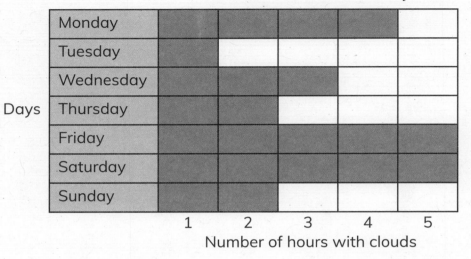

Days

Number of hours with clouds

a Complete the pictogram to show the same data.

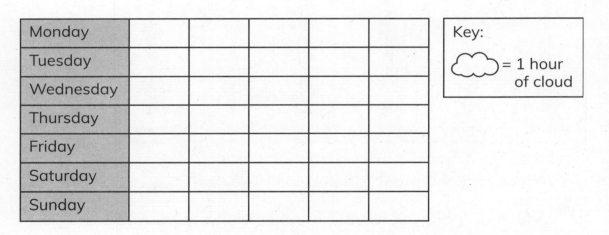

Monday					
Tuesday					
Wednesday					
Thursday					
Friday					
Saturday					
Sunday					

Key:

= 1 hour of cloud

b Write two questions about the data and the answers.

1 _____

_____

2 _____

_____

Practice

5   This is a pictogram to show how many goals were
    scored this season. Look at the key.

Number of goals scored this season

team A	⚽ ⚽ ⚽ ⚽ ⚽ ⚽
team B	⚽ ⚽
team C	⚽ ⚽ ⚽
team D	⚽ ⚽ ⚽ ⚽ ⚽ ⚽

Key:

⚽ = 2 goals

a   Which team scored the most goals? _____

b   How many did they score? _____

c   Which team scored the fewest goals?
    How many did they score?

    _____

d   How many goals were scored by team A and

    team B all together? _____

e   Write two questions with answers of your own.

    1   _____

        _____

    2   _____

        _____

6   This is the bar chart.

Make up your own title for it.

Write your own labels and numbers on the axes.

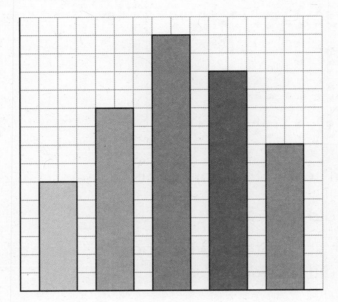

Write two questions for someone else to answer.

1   _____

    _____

2   _____

    _____

7   a   Show this pictogram as a bar chart.

Number of trees planted each week

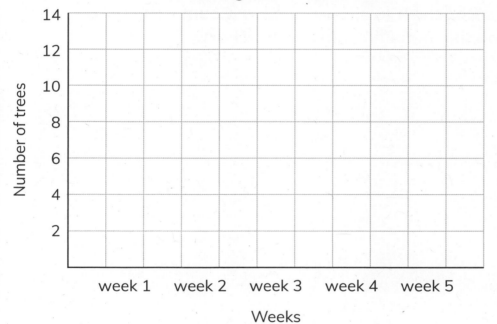

b   Write two questions about the data in the graphs.

1   _____

    _____

2   _____

    _____

Challenge

8   The ice cream seller does a survey to find the most
     popular ice cream flavour.

     •   12 like vanilla.

     •   Three more than that like chocolate.

     •   Six like strawberry.

     •   11 like lemon.

     •   The favourite flavour is mint. It has the same
          number as strawberry and lemon together.

     Make a bar chart to show the data. Count up in twos.
     Add the title and labels to the bar chart.

9 Use the data about the vehicles to complete the pictogram.

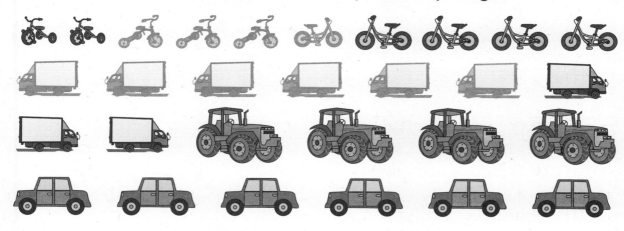

Title:	

Key
1 picture = 1 vehicle

🚲	
🚲	
🚲	
🚲	
🚚	
🚚	
🚜	
🚗	

a   How many vehicles are there all together?

There are _____ cars.

There are _____ tractors.

There are _____ trucks.

There are _____ bikes.

There are _____ trikes.

b   Is the number of cars greater than the number of trucks?

_____

What is the difference between them?

_____

c   What is the difference between the number of trikes and the number of tractors?

_____

10 Write a title and a key for this pictogram. Label the two axes.

Title:

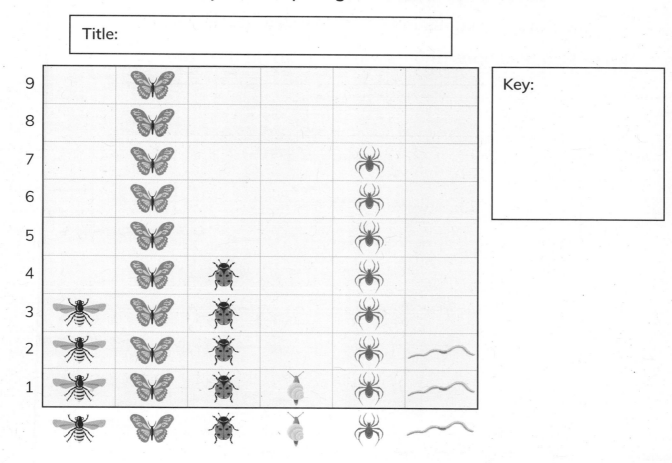

Key:

11 Write a title for this bar chart.

Use the data from question 10 to complete the bar chart.

Write two questions and the answers about the data.

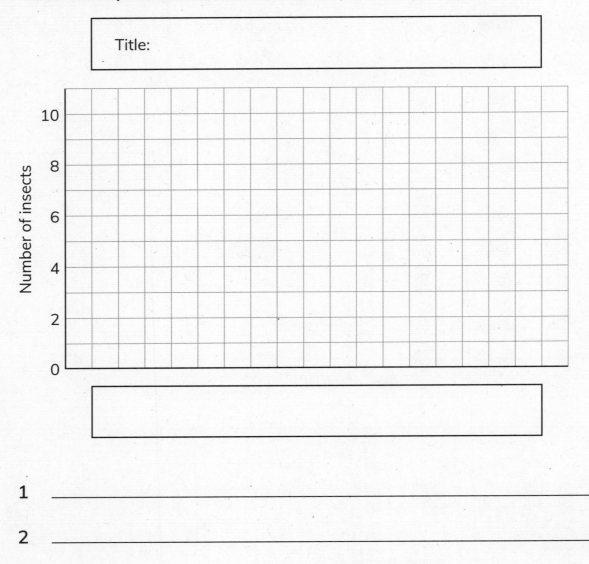

Title:

Number of insects

10

8

6

4

2

0

1 _____

2 _____

> 10.2 Venn and Carroll diagrams

Exercise 10.2

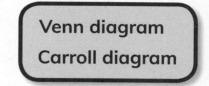

Venn diagram

Carroll diagram

Worked example 2

How can these numbers be sorted into a
Venn diagram?

19   13   22   11   12   28   15   17   14   26   24

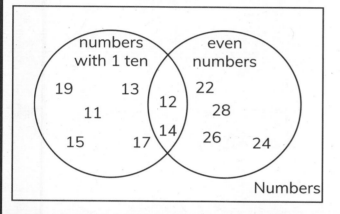

Look at the tens digit. Look at the ones digit.

If these numbers are sorted into this Venn diagram,
it would look like this.

24   35   28   14   38   30   12   37   39   32

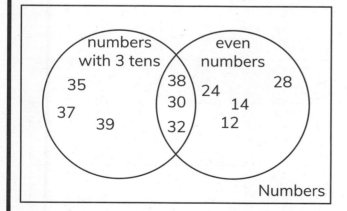

The space in the middle is for numbers that follow both rules.

Focus

1   Sort these numbers into the Venn diagram.

14   5   56   82   61   7   41   9   45   68   72   3

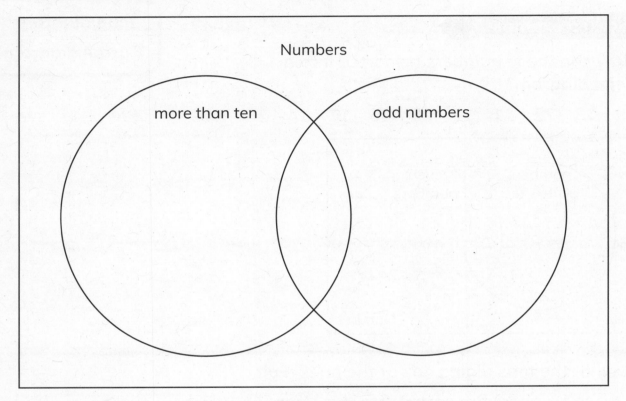

2   Put the following numbers into the correct place on
    the Carroll diagram.

    Cross out the numbers as you use them.

    1, 2, 5, 10, 14, 15, 21, 27, 35, 47, 55, 62, 76, 83, 91, 108

	1-digit numbers	not 1-digit numbers
even numbers		
not even numbers		

3   You are designing a new school uniform. You can choose between:

- green or yellow

- a t-shirt or a shirt.

Write down two questions to ask other learners.

1 _____

2 _____

How will you record the data? Ask up to ten other learners
and record your data here.

Now show your data in a way that is clear and easy to read.

> **Tip**
>
> What ways do you know to show data? Think about the
> advantages and disadvantages of each way, to help you
> decide what to choose.

Draw the school uniform you have chosen and explain your choice.

Practice

4 a Draw lines to sort these 2D shapes on this Venn diagram.

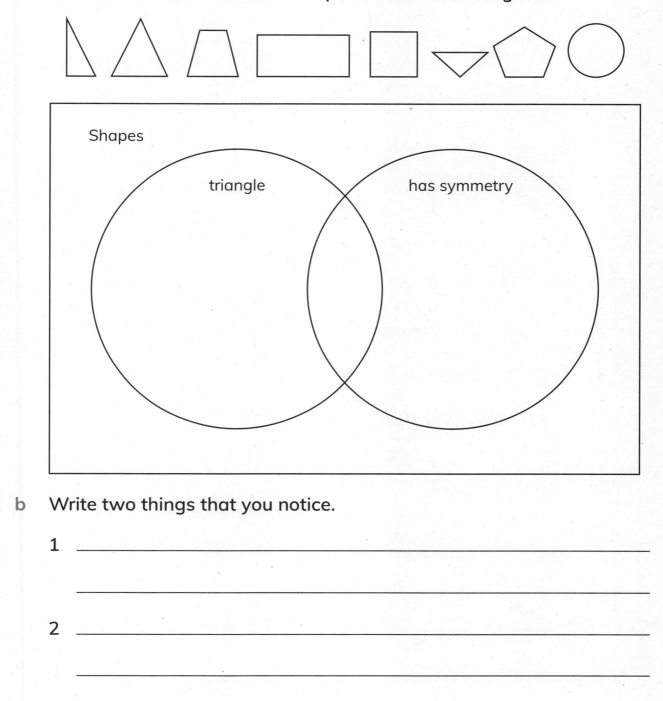

b Write two things that you notice.

1 _____

_____

2 _____

_____

5   Look at the numbers.

245   106   17   4   71   912   13   555   56   45   18

a   Put them in the correct boxes in the Carroll diagram.

	less than 50	not less than 50
odd		
not odd		

b   Choose a number and write it in the Carroll diagram.

More than 50 and odd: _____

Less than 50 and even: _____

Less than 50 and odd: _____

More than 50 and even: _____

6   Write the data to complete the Carroll diagram.

66   50   45   69   24   55   60   18   20   68   97

	÷ 3	does not ÷ 3
÷ 5		
does not ÷ 5		

7   Imagine you own a pet shop. You are deciding what pet food to sell.
    You only have space for three different types of pet food.

    Write down questions to ask people to help you decide what
    pet food to sell.

    _____

    _____

    How will you record the data? Ask up to ten people and record
    your data here.

    Now show your data in a way that is clear and easy to read.

    Tip

    What ways do you know to show data? Think about the
    advantages and disadvantages of each way, to help you
    decide what to choose.

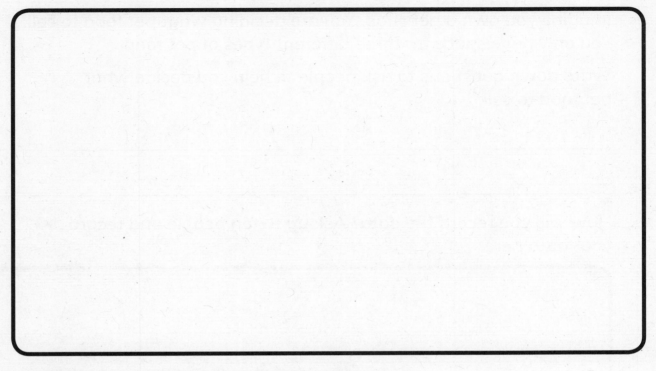

Write down three things your data tells you.

1 _____

2 _____

3 _____

What pet food will you sell? Explain your choice.

_____

_____

Challenge

8   The labels are missing from this Venn diagram.

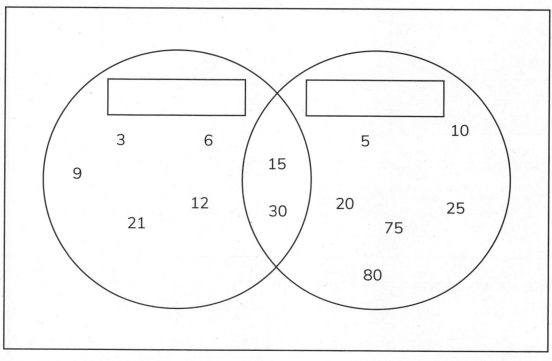

a   Write the labels.

b   What would you write in the box? Explain why.

_____

_____

c   Add these numbers to the Venn diagram:
    13, 14, 16, 17, 18, 19, 45.

d   Explain why some numbers are outside the circles.

_____

_____

9 a Put numbers 10 to 40 in the correct place in this
      Carroll diagram.

	Between 10 and 20	Not between 10 and 20
Digits add to an even number		
Digits do not add to an even number		

   b Explain how you knew where to place the numbers.

      _____

      _____

10 a Write labels in the Carroll diagram.

	107, 156, 235	140, 490
	18, 24, 51, 6	30, 50, 20

b   Use the data to complete the Venn diagram.

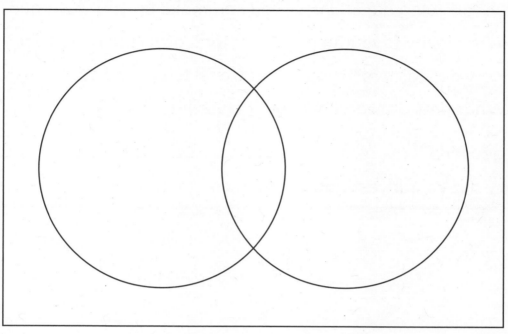

11 a   How are bar charts and pictograms different?

_____

_____

b   Which would be better to represent this information,
a bar chart or a pictogram? Explain why.

Child	Number of jumps in a minute
Hamzid	24
Kara	18
Toby	15
Gabby	21

_____

_____

c   Carry out your own investigation. You can choose to investigate any of the following questions or you can make up your own question:

- What is the favourite breakfast for learners in your class?
- How do learners in your class travel to school?
- What pets do learners in your class have?

My question is _____

Carry out your investigation and record your data.

Decide how to present the data you collected.
Present your data below.

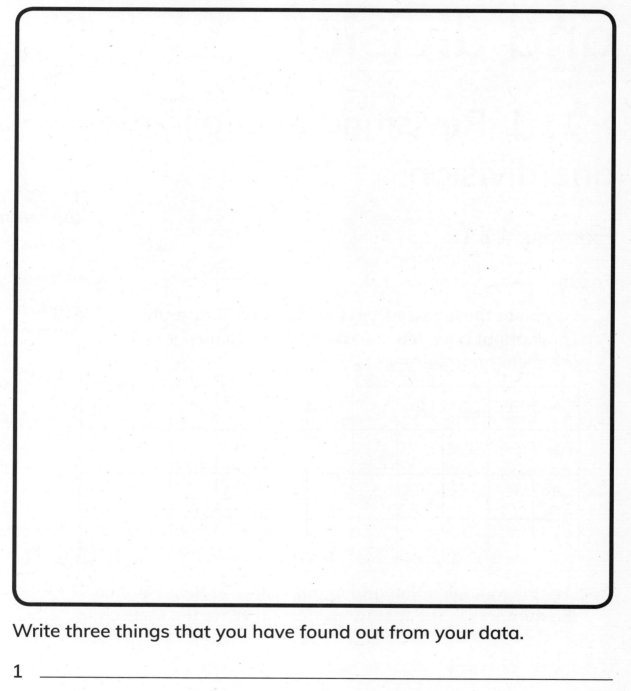

Write three things that you have found out from your data.

1 _____

2 _____

3 _____

11 More multiplication and division

> 11.1 Revisiting multiplication and division

Exercise 11.1

Focus

commutative
diagonal line
extend
product

1   Complete these rows from the multiplication square. Think about how you can use one row to help you complete another row.

×	1	2	3	4	5	6	7	8	9	10
2										
4										
8										

2   Use the multiplication grid in question 1 to help you find the numbers in the fact family for 32. Write the fact family.

_____

_____

_____

3   Extend each sequence. What is the term-to-term rule for each sequence?

a   8, 12, 16, 20, ☐ , ☐ , ☐ .

The term-to-term rule is _____ .

b   26, 31, 36, 41, ☐ , ☐ , ☐ .

The term-to-term rule is _____ .

c   27, 24, 21, 18, ☐ , ☐ , ☐ .

The term-to-term rule is _____ .

Practice

4   Complete these rows from the multiplication square.
Think about how you can use one row to help you
complete another row.

×	1	2	3	4	5	6	7	8	9	10
3										
6										
9										

5   Find the product 24 in the grid in question 4. Read along the row and
column from each product to find the group size and quotient for a
division calculation. Write the four division calculations that you find.

_____

_____

6   Which eight numbers are repeated four times each in
    the 10 by 10 multiplication square to 10 × 10?
    Why are these numbers repeated so often?

7   Choose a number that is included in the multiplication
    grid twice. Write its fact family.

Challenge

8   Which numbers are included three times in the multiplication grid?
    Explain why.

    _____

    _____

    _____

9   Sanjay wonders why there is no zero row or column on
    the multiplication square. Explain why to Sanjay.

    _____

    _____

10 Jinghua wants to write a sequence with the term-to-term
    rule − 9. Where could she look on the multiplication square
    to get started?

    _____

    _____

11 17 and 29 are two of the numbers in a sequence.
    What could the sequence be? What is the term-to-term rule?

> 11.2 Playing with multiplication and division

Exercise 11.2

Focus

distributive   quotient
remainder   simplify

1   Multiply each set of three numbers in any order
    to simplify the calculation and find the product.

    a   2 × 3 × 5 _____   b   4 × 5 × 6 _____

    c   5 × 5 × 4 _____   d   9 × 3 × 2 _____

Tip

Remember,
multiplication is
commutative,
you can multiply
numbers together
in any order
you choose.

2   Complete these simplified multiplications.

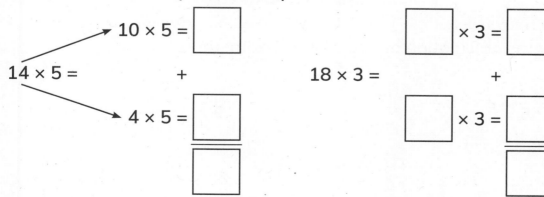

10 × 5 = ☐

14 × 5 =   +

4 × 5 = ☐

☐ × 3 = ☐

18 × 3 =   +

☐ × 3 = ☐

3   Complete each division. Make sure you include any remainders.
    You could use counters to help you.

a   20 ÷ 2 = ▢   b   20 ÷ 3 = ▢

c   20 ÷ 4 = ▢   d   20 ÷ 5 = ▢

Practice

4   a   Choose three single-digit numbers to multiply together
        to make an easy calculation. Find the product.

        ▢ × ▢ × ▢ = ▢

    b   Choose three single-digit numbers to multiply together
        to make a difficult calculation. Find the product.

        ▢ × ▢ × ▢ = ▢

        What makes this calculation difficult?

        _____

        _____

5   Find each product.
    Simplify the calculation or use a different method.

a   11 × 5 =   b   19 × 2 =

c $13 \times 3 =$

d $15 \times 4 =$

6   Find at least three different solutions to this division
    calculation. The ☐ and △ represent the unknown values.

    $25 \div \square = \triangle \, r1$

7   Six children share a bag of 50 sweets between them
    equally. How many sweets does each child get?

    Write the division calculation that shows the result.

Challenge

8   Three different numbers from 2 to 10 are multiplied together.
    The product is 120. What could the numbers be?
    Find two different solutions.

9   Complete the multiplication grid using any method that you choose.

×	13	16	19
3			
4			
5			

10   A school orders 60 glue sticks to be shared
     equally between five classes. When the glue
     sticks arrive, three extra free glue sticks have
     been added to the box.

     Write the division calculation to show how
     the school shares the glue sticks.

11   A division calculation has a remainder of 8.
     What does this tell you about the calculation?

_____

_____

12 Complete each division calculation.

a ☐ ÷ 2 = 7 r1

b ☐ ÷ 3 = 4 r2

c ☐ ÷ 4 = 7 r2

d ☐ ÷ 3 = 9 r1

e ☐ ÷ 10 = 7 r6

f ☐ ÷ 9 = 4 r3

> 11.3 Extending multiplication and division

Exercise 11.3

Focus

approach

interpret

1 Estimate the product of 27 × 5. Record the multiplication calculation in a grid and find the product.

estimate:

2 Complete this division calculation.

86 ÷ 4 =

Estimate: 80 ÷ 4 = 20. So 86 ÷ 4 must be a bit more than 20.

$$\begin{array}{r} 86 \\ - \underline{40} \quad \text{10 groups of 4} \\ 46 \end{array}$$

3 The bicycle maker has 19 wheels.
How many bicycles can she make?

4 Three children can sit at a small table.
How many small tables are needed for
37 children? Show your method.

Practice

5   Estimate and then find the product for each multiplication.

   a   estimate:

   $46 \times 5 =$

   b   estimate:

   $89 \times 2 =$

   c   estimate:

   $67 \times 3 =$

   d   estimate:

   $78 \times 4 =$

6   Estimate and then find the answer for each division.

   a   estimate:

   $53 \div 2 =$

   b   estimate:

   $91 \div 4 =$

c   estimate:

97 ÷ 3 = ☐

d   estimate:

74 ÷ 5 = ☐

7   The timber store is making three-legged stools.
    The store has 35 stool legs.
    How many stools can they make? Show your method.

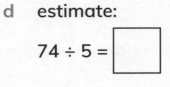

8   A taxi can carry four people and
    the taxi driver. Ten people want
    to go to a show. How many taxis
    do they need? Show your method.

Challenge

9   Choose which numbers in the grid to multiply by 2, 3, 4
    or 5 to find the smallest and greatest products. How do
    you know that you have found the smallest and
    greatest products? Remember to estimate the product
    before you multiply.

68	37	86
93	45	69
74	96	39

Smallest product:

estimate:

Greatest product:

estimate:

10 Using the numbers in the grid in question 9, choose a number to divide
    by 2, 3, 4 and 5. Remember to estimate before dividing.

    estimate:

11 I have $25. Computer games cost $4.
How many computer games can I buy?
How much change will I get?
Show your method.

12 How many 3 cm lengths of ribbon can be cut
from 1 metre of ribbon?
How long is the piece left over?
Show your method.

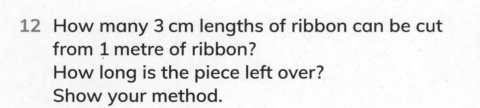

13 I am thinking of a number. I multiply it by 3 and add 2 to
get the answer 83. What is my number? Show your method.

12 > More fractions

> 12.1 Fractions of numbers

Exercise 12.1

Focus

1   A fraction strip is 20 cm long.
    Wunmi is marking quarters on the strip.

   a   Where should she mark $\frac{1}{4}$? At _____ cm.

   b   Where should she mark $\frac{2}{4}$? At _____ cm.

   c   Where should she mark $\frac{3}{4}$? At _____ cm.

2   a   Draw a (ring) around $\frac{1}{3}$ of the cubes.

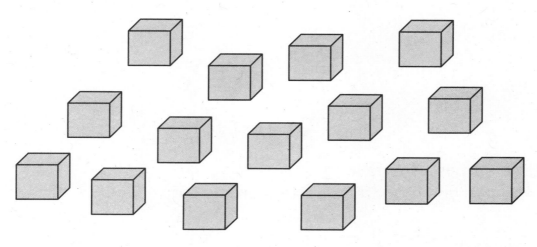

   b   What fraction of the cubes are **not** ringed? _____

3 Find these fractions of 12.

12	$\frac{1}{2}$	$\frac{1}{3}$	$\frac{1}{4}$	$\frac{1}{10}$	$\frac{3}{4}$
				X	

4 Find each fraction and complete the matching division calculation.

a $\frac{1}{2}$ of 6 = ☐ ,   6 ÷ ☐ = ☐

b $\frac{1}{4}$ of 16 = ☐ ,   16 ÷ ☐ = ☐

5 A new chocolate bar has three separate fingers. Four children want an equal share. How much does each child get? Draw a diagram to help you.

Practice

6 A fraction strip is 1 metre long.
Where should you mark the quarters on the strip?

a $\frac{1}{4}$ at _____ cm.   b $\frac{2}{4}$ at _____ cm.   c $\frac{3}{4}$ at _____ cm.

7 a What fraction of the cubes are ringed? _____

   b What fraction of the cubes are not ringed? _____

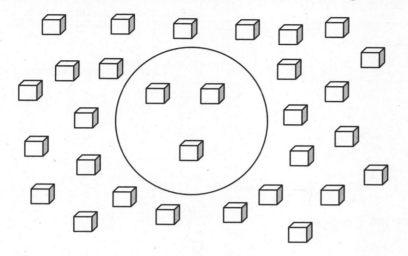

8 What is the whole in the table below?
   Complete the rest of the table.

___	$\frac{1}{2}$	$\frac{1}{3}$	$\frac{1}{4}$	$\frac{1}{10}$	$\frac{3}{4}$
					21

9 Complete each fraction statement and write the
   matching division calculations.

   a $\frac{1}{4}$ of ☐ = 12

   b $\frac{1}{2}$ of ☐ = 7

10 There are four tomatoes in a pack.
Kai uses two tomatoes.
What fraction of the tomatoes does he use?

Challenge

11 a A fraction strip has $\frac{1}{5}$ marked at 9 cm.

How long is the fraction strip?

_____

_____

b Where should $\frac{1}{3}$ be marked on this fraction strip?

_____

12 Zara and Sofia both made a fraction strip, but both strips
are torn. Whose strip was shorter? How do you know?

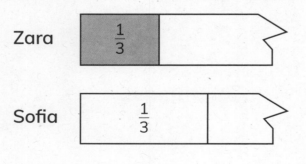

_____

_____

13 There are 24 marbles in $\frac{3}{4}$ of a bag of marbles.

How many marbles are in a full bag? Show your method.

14 Fatima buys a bunch of grapes.

She eats $\frac{1}{3}$ of the bunch.

There are 18 grapes left.
How many grapes were in the bunch that
Fatima bought? Show your method.

15 There are 12 nails in a pack.
Feng uses nine nails.
What fraction of the pack does he use?

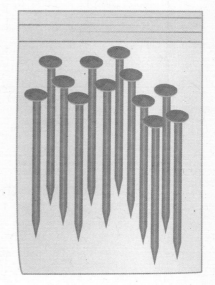

> 12.2 Ordering and comparing fractions

Exercise 12.2

inequality
multiple

Focus

1   Mark $\frac{1}{3}$ and $\frac{2}{3}$ on this number line.

0   1

2   Which fractions could be marked on a number line between 0 and $\frac{1}{4}$?

3   Use the fraction strips to help you compare $\frac{1}{4}$ and $\frac{1}{3}$.

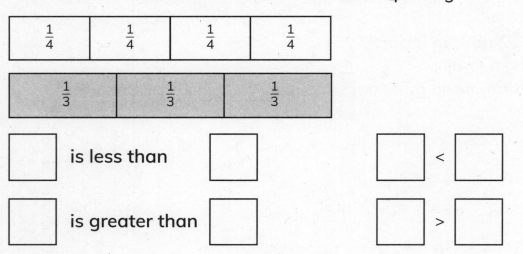

| $\frac{1}{4}$ | $\frac{1}{4}$ | $\frac{1}{4}$ | $\frac{1}{4}$ |

| $\frac{1}{3}$ | $\frac{1}{3}$ | $\frac{1}{3}$ |

☐ is less than ☐   ☐ < ☐

☐ is greater than ☐   ☐ > ☐

4   Use the fraction wall to help you order these fractions.

1									
$\frac{1}{2}$					$\frac{1}{2}$				
$\frac{1}{3}$			$\frac{1}{3}$			$\frac{1}{3}$			
$\frac{1}{4}$		$\frac{1}{4}$		$\frac{1}{4}$			$\frac{1}{4}$		
$\frac{1}{5}$		$\frac{1}{5}$		$\frac{1}{5}$		$\frac{1}{5}$		$\frac{1}{5}$	
$\frac{1}{10}$	$\frac{1}{10}$	$\frac{1}{10}$	$\frac{1}{10}$	$\frac{1}{10}$	$\frac{1}{10}$	$\frac{1}{10}$	$\frac{1}{10}$	$\frac{1}{10}$	$\frac{1}{10}$

a   Put these fractions in order from smallest to largest.

$\frac{1}{5}, \frac{1}{10}, \frac{1}{3}.$

_____

_____

b   Put these fractions in order from largest to smallest.

$\frac{4}{5}, \frac{2}{5}, \frac{3}{5}.$

_____

_____

Practice

5   Mark $\frac{5}{10}$, $\frac{7}{10}$ and $\frac{9}{10}$ on this 10 cm long number line.

0   1

6   Which fractions could be marked on a number line

between $\frac{1}{4}$ and $\frac{1}{2}$?

7   $\frac{1}{4}$ of Zara's ribbon is the same length as $\frac{1}{3}$ of Sofia's ribbon.

Whose ribbon is shorter? How do you know?

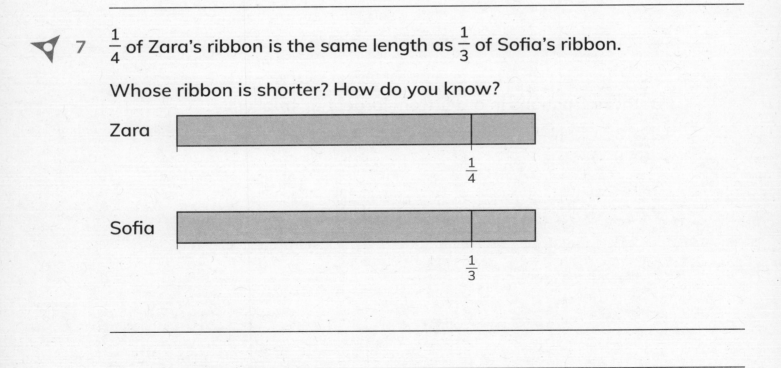

8   Which fraction will give you the larger amount?

a $\frac{1}{3}$ or $\frac{1}{10}$ of a cake?   b $\frac{2}{4}$ or $\frac{3}{4}$ of \$2?

c $\frac{5}{5}$ or $\frac{1}{5}$ of a pizza?

9   a   Use the fraction strips to help you compare $\frac{1}{10}$ and $\frac{1}{5}$.

| $\frac{1}{10}$ | $\frac{1}{10}$ | $\frac{1}{10}$ | $\frac{1}{10}$ | $\frac{1}{10}$ | $\frac{1}{10}$ | $\frac{1}{10}$ | $\frac{1}{10}$ | $\frac{1}{10}$ | $\frac{1}{10}$ |

| $\frac{1}{5}$ | $\frac{1}{5}$ | $\frac{1}{5}$ | $\frac{1}{5}$ | $\frac{1}{5}$ |

☐   is less than   ☐   ☐ < ☐

☐   is greater than   ☐   ☐ > ☐

b   What do you notice about fifths and tenths?

_____

_____

Challenge

10 Order each set of fractions from largest to smallest:

a $\dfrac{1}{5}$, $\dfrac{1}{4}$, $\dfrac{1}{10}$, $\dfrac{1}{2}$, $\dfrac{1}{3}$.

_____

b $\dfrac{3}{10}$, $\dfrac{6}{10}$, $\dfrac{10}{10}$, $\dfrac{9}{10}$, $\dfrac{7}{10}$.

_____

11 Use <, > or = to complete each statement.

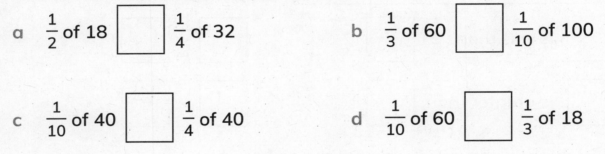

a $\dfrac{1}{2}$ of 18 ☐ $\dfrac{1}{4}$ of 32   b $\dfrac{1}{3}$ of 60 ☐ $\dfrac{1}{10}$ of 100

c $\dfrac{1}{10}$ of 40 ☐ $\dfrac{1}{4}$ of 40   d $\dfrac{1}{10}$ of 60 ☐ $\dfrac{1}{3}$ of 18

12 Write two fractions that are larger than $\dfrac{1}{3}$.

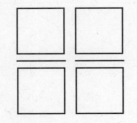

> 12.3 Calculating with fractions

Exercise 12.3

Focus

original

reduced

1 What addition is shown on this diagram?

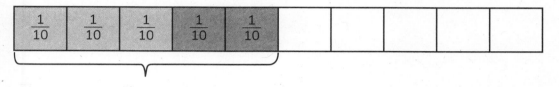

2 Complete the numerators to make this calculation correct.
Find three different solutions.

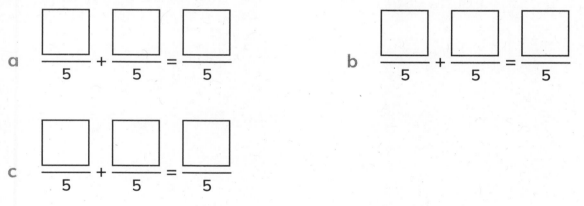

a $\dfrac{\square}{5} + \dfrac{\square}{5} = \dfrac{\square}{5}$

b $\dfrac{\square}{5} + \dfrac{\square}{5} = \dfrac{\square}{5}$

c $\dfrac{\square}{5} + \dfrac{\square}{5} = \dfrac{\square}{5}$

3 What subtraction is shown on this diagram?

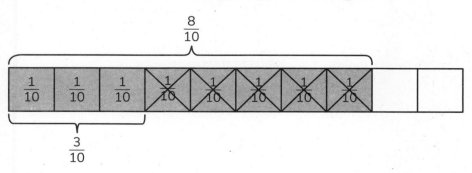

4 A television programme lasts for $\frac{1}{3}$ of an hour.

How many minutes is that?

Practice

5 Use diagrams or fraction strips to help you complete each calculation.
Estimate before you calculate.
Draw a (ring) around your estimate.

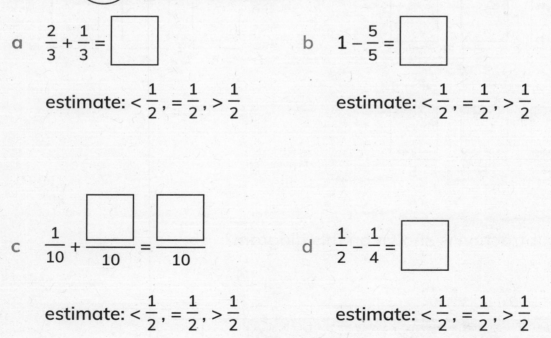

a $\frac{2}{3} + \frac{1}{3} = \boxed{}$

estimate: $< \frac{1}{2}$, $= \frac{1}{2}$, $> \frac{1}{2}$

b $1 - \frac{5}{5} = \boxed{}$

estimate: $< \frac{1}{2}$, $= \frac{1}{2}$, $> \frac{1}{2}$

c $\frac{1}{10} + \frac{\boxed{}}{10} = \frac{\boxed{}}{10}$

estimate: $< \frac{1}{2}$, $= \frac{1}{2}$, $> \frac{1}{2}$

d $\frac{1}{2} - \frac{1}{4} = \boxed{}$

estimate: $< \frac{1}{2}$, $= \frac{1}{2}$, $> \frac{1}{2}$

6 Find all the possible solutions for this calculation.

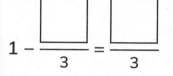

$$1 - \frac{\boxed{}}{3} = \frac{\boxed{}}{3}$$

7 Mariposa buys a T-shirt in the sale.
Its price was $30 originally,

but the price is now reduced by $\frac{1}{3}$.

How much does Mariposa pay for the T-shirt?

$30

Challenge

8 Hien mixes 200 millilitres of orange juice,
200 millilitres of pineapple juice and
200 millilitres of lemonade.
What fraction of a litre is the drink
that he makes?

9 Use diagrams or fraction strips to help you check each calculation.
Tick (✓) the correct answers.
If the calculation is incorrect, correct it.

a $\dfrac{5}{10} + \dfrac{4}{10} = \dfrac{9}{10}$

b $\dfrac{5}{5} - \dfrac{1}{5} = \dfrac{3}{5}$

c $\dfrac{3}{4} - \dfrac{1}{4} = \dfrac{1}{2}$

d $\dfrac{3}{3} - \dfrac{0}{3} = \dfrac{0}{3}$

e $\dfrac{10}{10} - \dfrac{3}{10} = \dfrac{1}{10}$

10 Inaya buys 20 metres of fabric to make some curtains.

She uses $\dfrac{9}{10}$ of the fabric. How much fabric is left?

13 Measures

> 13.1 Mass

Exercise 13.1

gram (g)

kilogram (kg)

mass

Worked example 1

If the apple has a mass of 70 g, what is the mass of the pear?

160 g

160 g – 70 g = 90 g

The pear has a mass of 90 g.

The total mass of the apple and the pear is 160 g. To find the mass of the pear, take away the mass of the apple.

Focus

1 a What is the mass of this parcel rounded to the nearest 100 g? _____

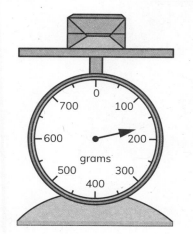

b   What is the mass of the chick rounded to the

nearest 10 g? _____

2   Zara, Arun and Sofia are finding out the mass of
the potatoes and the flour.

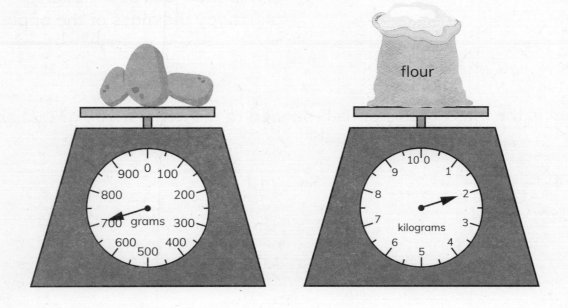

The potatoes have more mass because the arrow is further around the scale than the flour.

Zara

The flour has less mass because 2 kg is less than 700 g.

Arun

The flour has more mass because 2 kg is more than 700 g.

Sofia

Who is correct? Explain your answer.

_____

_____

3   Estimate and ⟨ring⟩ the mass of each object.

a   Carrot   8 kg   4 kg   18 g

b   Sheep   9 kg   90 kg   900 g

c   Feather   1 g   50 g   1 kg

d   Frog   3 g   30 g   3 kg

Practice

4   If the skin has a mass of 850 g, how much melon can be eaten?

Tip

Change 3 kg to grams. Remember, 1 kg is the same as 1000 g.

Show how you worked out the answer.

5 Write the mass that is showing on each scale. Round
   each reading up or down, to the nearest 100 grams.

a
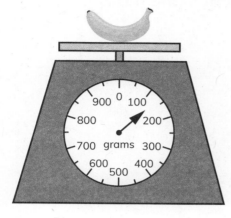

_____

b

_____

c

_____

6 Estimate and then (ring) the mass of each object.

a	A rabbit has a mass of about	10 g	100 g	1 kg.
b	A pumpkin has a mass of about	700 g	3 kg	13 kg.
c	A cell phone has a mass of about	2 kg	1 g	140 g.

Challenge

7   a   If one parcel has a mass of 900 g, what is the mass

of the other parcel? _____

3 kg

b   Draw scales that show more than 1 kg.

c   Draw three parcels. One has a mass of less than
500 g, one has a mass of between 600 g and 950 g
and the last one can be your choice.

Label the parcels.

Write a question of your own and its answer.

_____

_____

_____

8   Round up or down the readings, to the nearest whole number.

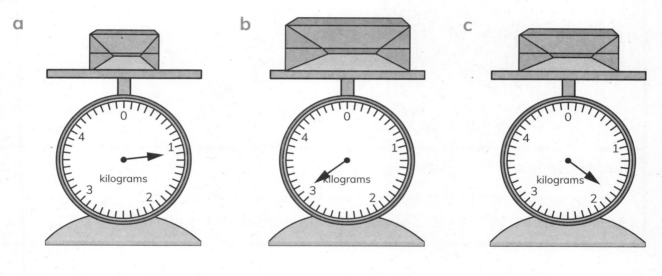

a   b   c

_____   _____   _____

9   The potatoes weigh 7 kilograms, rounded to the nearest whole number. The arrow is missing from the scale. Colour in all parts of the scale that the arrow could point to and still be rounded to 7 kilograms.

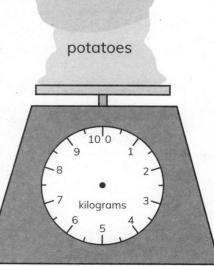

> 13.2 Capacity

Exercise 13.2

capacity   litres (l)

millilitres (ml)

Worked example 2

The sheep farmer has a full 5 litre bucket of water.

Each lamb needs 500 ml of water.

Does the farmer have enough water?

Yes, she does.

One lamb will have half a litre. Two lambs will have 1 litre.
So four lambs will have 2 litres and six lambs will have 3 litres.

Focus

1   Three friends want a drink of water. They have a
    bottle of water that holds 2 litres. The bottle is full.

    Each friend also has a cup. Each cup has
    the capacity to hold 500 ml of water.

    Can they all have a drink?
    Explain how you know.

Tip

Remember, 1 litre is
the same as 1000 ml.

_____

_____

2   Each container has a different capacity.
    Write the amount held in each container, to the nearest 100 ml.

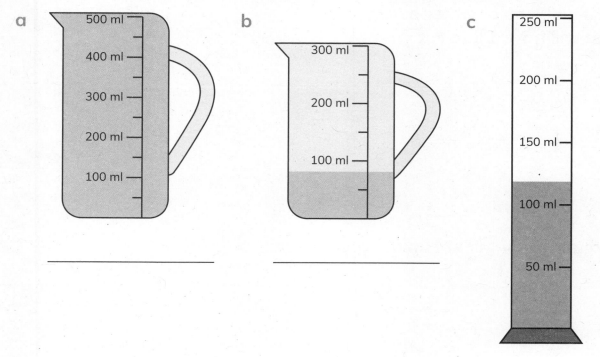

a
b
c

_____   _____   _____

d   This jug has the capacity to hold 3 litres of liquid.
    Fill this jug to two and a half litres.

3   The capacity of the jug is 2 litres.
    Nadine estimates that if she
    pours 500 ml of water away,
    she will have 1 litre left.

What do you think? Explain your answer.

_____

_____

Practice

4   My flask has the full capacity of 400 ml of water.
    Show how you worked out your answers.

    a   I pour out half. How many millilitres did I pour out?

        _____

    b   I pour out a quarter of 400 ml. How much is left in my flask?

        _____

    c   I pour out three-quarters of 400 ml. How much is left in my flask?

        _____

5   Each of these containers has a capacity of 1 litre. They are not all full.

Use the clues to find out who has which container.

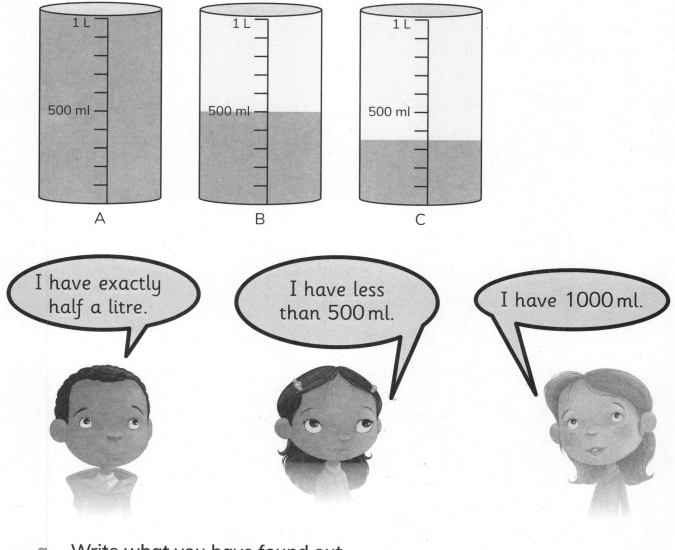

a   Write what you have found out.

_____

_____

_____

6   Khoa has put juice in each of these jugs.
    Each jug has a capacity of 1 litre.

    Khoa estimates that if he pours three more drinks using
    jug 2, both jugs will have the same amount of juice in them.
    Each drink is 125 ml.

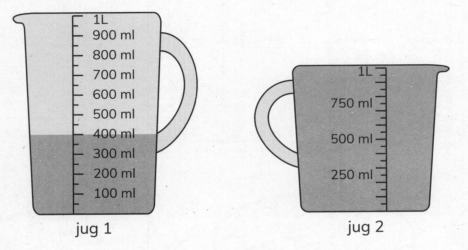

jug 1   jug 2

Is he right? _____

How much juice will be left in jug 2?

_____

Challenge

7   True or false:

The tallest container always has the largest capacity.

Is that statement correct?

Explain your reasons and draw examples.

_____

_____

8   I bought a full bottle of water with a capacity of 1 litre.
    I poured one-quarter of a 1 litre bottle of water into a glass.

a   How many millilitres are left in the bottle? _____

b   What fraction is left in the bottle? _____

c   If I had poured out three-quarters of a full bottle,

    how many millilitres is that? _____

d   How many millilitres would have been left in the bottle? _____

> 13.3 Temperature

Exercise 13.3

Celsius (C)
degree (°)

Worked example 3

This water has just started boiling. Look at the thermometer.
What temperature is boiling water?

The black line shows 100 °C. Water boils at 100 °C.

Temperature is measured in degrees Celsius.

Focus

1   The thermometer is in ice.

    a   What temperature does it show?

    _____

    b   What is the difference between the
        temperature of the ice and the temperature
        of boiling water?

    _____

2 a Which thermometer shows the coldest temperature? _____

   b Which thermometer shows the warmest temperature? _____

   c What is the temperature on thermometer C? _____

   d Which two thermometers are above 20 °C? _____

A 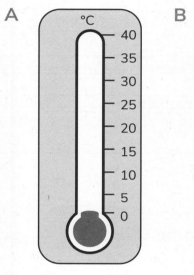 B 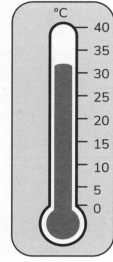 C 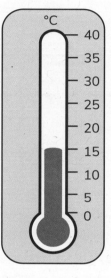 D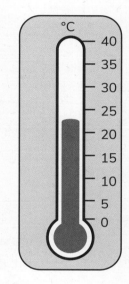

   e Use this thermometer to show the temperature that
      you like best. Do you like to be hot, warm or cold?

      I like to be _____ because _____.

3 **a** Round the temperature up or down, to the nearest number on the scale.

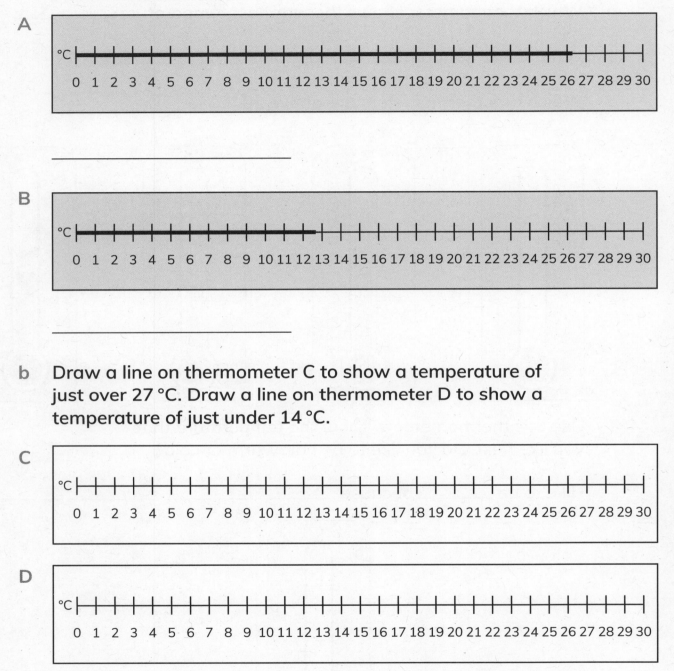

A
°C 0 1 2 3 4 5 6 7 8 9 10 11 12 13 14 15 16 17 18 19 20 21 22 23 24 25 26 27 28 29 30

_____

B
°C 0 1 2 3 4 5 6 7 8 9 10 11 12 13 14 15 16 17 18 19 20 21 22 23 24 25 26 27 28 29 30

_____

b Draw a line on thermometer C to show a temperature of just over 27 °C. Draw a line on thermometer D to show a temperature of just under 14 °C.

C
°C 0 1 2 3 4 5 6 7 8 9 10 11 12 13 14 15 16 17 18 19 20 21 22 23 24 25 26 27 28 29 30

D
°C 0 1 2 3 4 5 6 7 8 9 10 11 12 13 14 15 16 17 18 19 20 21 22 23 24 25 26 27 28 29 30

c   For each reading, round up or down to the nearest number.

Thermometer A is rounded _____ to _____ °C.

Thermometer B is rounded _____ to _____ °C.

Thermometer C is rounded _____ to _____ °C.

Thermometer D is rounded _____ to _____ °C.

Practice

4   a   What is the difference between the temperature in ice and the temperature of the air?

_____

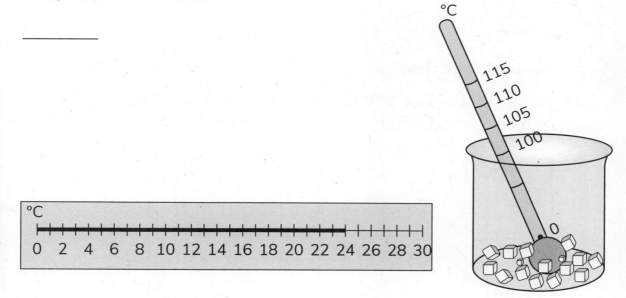

b   Look at the temperatures shown in the table.
    This table shows the temperature on the same day
    but in two different countries.

Month	Country A	Country B
April	9 °C	31 °C
May	12 °C	31 °C
June	17 °C	32 °C
July	18 °C	33 °C

Write the difference between the temperatures in the
two countries in:

June _____   April _____   July _____   May _____

c   Which month has the biggest temperature difference? _____

5   a   House plants like a temperature that is just over 18 °C.
        Which thermometer shows the best temperature for the plants? _____

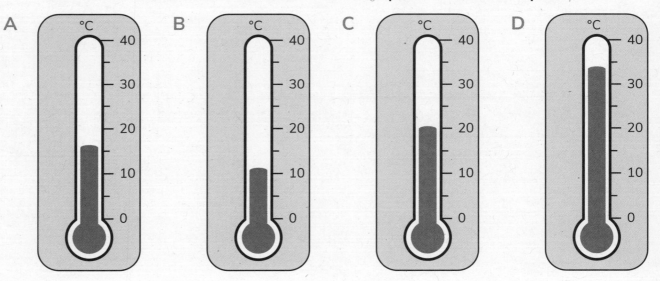

b   What temperature does it show? _____

c   In school, temperatures should not fall below 15 °C.
Show and write a temperature that would close schools.

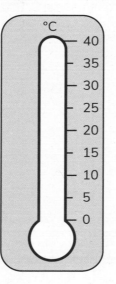

6   This thermometer is marked to show each 5 °C.

a   Write all of the missing marks.

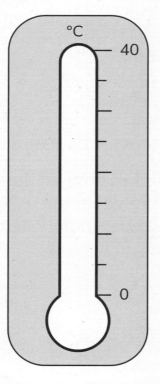

b   Show a temperature of more than 15 °C but less than 20 °C.

_____

Challenge

7 a Look at these two thermometers. Then fill in the gaps.

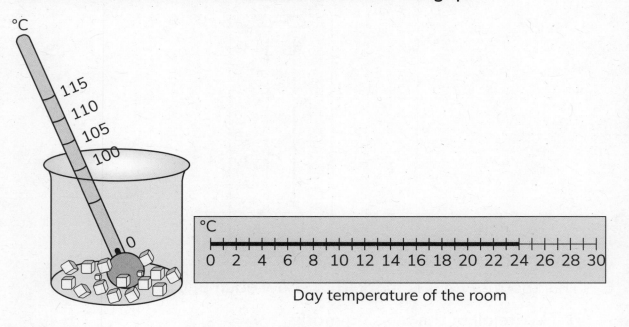

Day temperature of the room

The temperature of the _____ is higher than

the temperature of the _____.

b The night air temperature is 14 °C lower than the day

temperature. The temperature at night is _____.

c Water boils at 100 °C. Show on the thermometer
the new temperature when the temperature of
the water is 30 °C lower than boiling.

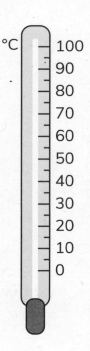

8   Compare the thermometers. (These pictures show only the
     top part of each thermometer.)

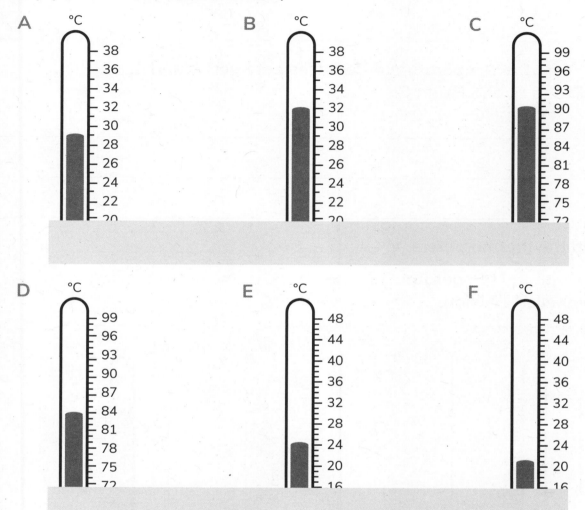

a   Draw a (ring) around the correct answer.

     Thermometer A shows a higher/lower temperature
     than thermometer B.

     Thermometer C shows a higher/lower temperature
     than thermometer D.

     Thermometer E shows a higher/lower temperature
     than thermometer F.

b Write the temperatures that each thermometer shows, rounding to the nearest labelled division.

A _____ B _____ C _____ D _____ E _____ F _____

c Write the temperature differences between A and E, D and B, and F and C.

_____

_____

_____

9 Read the thermometers.

a Write the temperatures in the boxes, rounding to the nearest labelled division.

°C

°C

°C

°C

°C

°C

°C

°C

°C

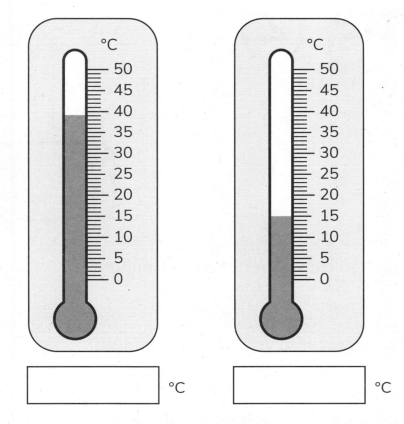

°C   °C

b   Write the temperatures from the warmest to the coldest.

_____

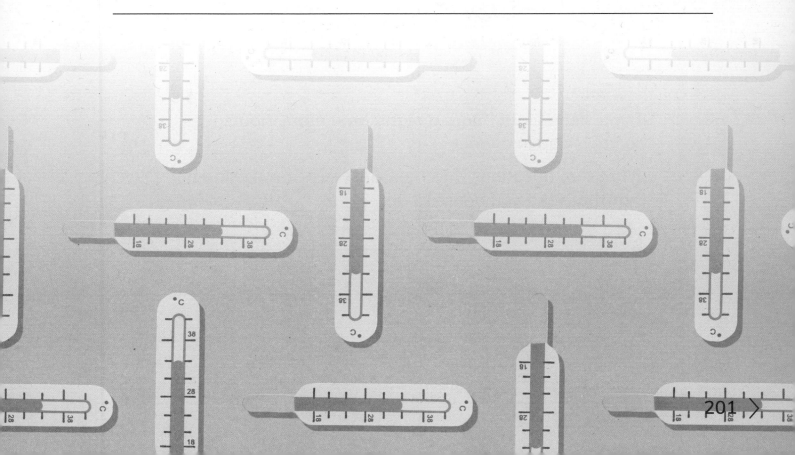

14 ▶ Time (2)

> 14.1 Time

Exercise 14.1

time

time interval

Focus

1 a How many times can you clap your hands in 1 minute?

   estimate = _____   measure = _____

   b How many times can you stamp your feet in 1 minute?

   estimate = _____   measure = _____

   c Write three things that would take more than a minute to do.

   1 _____

   2 _____

   3 _____

2 a If you sleep eight hours a night, how many hours
      do you sleep in a week?

   b Write two questions and their answers about things
      that that take you hours to do.

   1 _____

      _____

   2 _____

      _____

3   Use the calendar to find the answers.

| April |||||||
M	T	W	T	F	S	S
		1	2	3	4	5
6	7	8	9	10	11	12
13	14	15	16	17	18	19
20	21	22	23	24	25	26
27	28	29	30			

| May |||||||
M	T	W	T	F	S	S
				1	2	3
4	5	6	7	8	9	10
11	12	13	14	15	16	17
18	19	20	21	22	23	24
25	26	27	28	29	30	31

| June |||||||
M	T	W	T	F	S	S
1	2	3	4	5	6	7
8	9	10	11	12	13	14
15	16	17	18	19	20	21
22	23	24	25	26	27	28
29	30					

a   Raul planned a holiday to last two weeks.
He left on 15th May. When did he arrive home?

_____

b   Schools will close for a holiday on 14th April.
Learners will go back to school 20 days later.
What date do they go back to school?

_____

c   Four weeks after 3rd May is my birthday.
    What date is that?

    _____

d   My dentist appointment was on 24th June.
    I was asked to go two weeks earlier.
    When did I go to my appointment?

    _____

Practice

4   a   Choose from the choices in the boxes to estimate the length
        of time each of these activities would take.

1 hour	1 minute	less than 1 minute	more than 1 minute

one clap _____

walk around your classroom _____

stamp your foot _____

blink your eyes _____

math lesson _____

travel to school _____

get dressed _____

eat your breakfast _____

    b   What would take you more than an hour to do?

    _____

5 I was born in April 1999. My sister was born in
   March 1996.

March 1996						
M	T	W	T	F	S	S
				1	2	3
4	5	6	7	8	9	10
11	12	13	14	15	16	17
18	19	20	21	22	23	24
25	26	27	28	29	30	31

April 1999						
M	T	W	T	F	S	S
			1	2	3	4
5	6	7	8	9	10	11
12	13	14	15	16	17	18
19	20	21	22	23	24	25
26	27	28	29	30		

a   Our birthdays are both on the 26th.
    How many days apart are they?

    _____

b   My brother was born in 2007, nine days after
    my birthday. What day was he born?

    _____

c   How much older is my sister than my brother?

    _____

6 Use the calendar to help you solve these problems.

June						
M	T	W	T	F	S	S
1	2	3	4	5	6	7
8	9	10	11	12	13	14
15	16	17	18	19	20	21
22	23	24	25	26	27	28
29	30					

a   A bag of bird food lasts six days.
You opened the packet on Thursday 4th.
When will you open the next bag?

_____

b   I planned to visit the zoo on the 30th but went
two weeks earlier. When did I go?

_____

Challenge

7   a   Choose from the choices to estimate how long it takes:

to shake hands with a friend _____

to eat your breakfast _____

to walk around the outside of your school building _____

for the grass to grow 5 cm _____

b Write one more thing for each of these time units.

minutes: _____

hours: _____

days: _____

weeks: _____

8

November						
M	T	W	T	F	S	S
						1
2	3	4	5	6	7	8
9	10	11	12	13	14	15
16	17	18	19	20	21	22
23	24	25	26	27	28	29
30						

December						
M	T	W	T	F	S	S
	1	2	3	4	5	6
7	8	9	10	11	12	13
14	15	16	17	18	19	20
21	22	23	24	25	26	27
28	29	30	31			

January						
M	T	W	T	F	S	S
			1	2	3	4
5	6	7	8	9	10	11
12	13	14	15	16	17	18
19	20	21	22	23	24	25
26	27	28	29	30	31	

a Find two days and dates that are 17 days apart.

_____

_____

b Marsile, Mustafa and Majak went camping.
Marsile left on 9th November, Mustafa left on
12th November and Majak left on 27th November.
They all came home on 6th December.
How long was each boy away camping?

Marsile: Mustafa: Majak:

c Mustafa went camping again six weeks after he came
home on 6th December and he stayed 11 days.
Which day did he go and when did he come home?

_____

_____

9 **a** Anna was away for 13 days. Write two possible
pairs of dates for when she left and came back.

			August			
M	T	W	T	F	S	S
					1	2
3	4	5	6	7	8	9
10	11	12	13	14	15	16
17	18	19	20	21	22	23
24	25	26	27	28	29	30
31						

1 _____

2 _____

b Javed was away for 17 days. Write two possible pairs of dates for when he left and came back.

1 _____

_____

2 _____

_____

May						
M	T	W	T	F	S	S
				1	2	3
4	5	6	7	8	9	10
11	12	13	14	15	16	17
18	19	20	21	22	23	24
25	26	27	28	29	30	31

> 14.2 Timetables

Exercise 14.2

timetable

Worked example 1

This timetable shows a day at the seaside.

Play games	Eat lunch	Walk	Swim
11 a.m – 12 p.m.	12 – 1 p.m.	1.30 – 2 p.m.	2.15 – 3 p.m.

a Is the walk in the morning or afternoon?

b What time does lunch end?

c What are people doing at 3.00 pm?

a	Afternoon	The walk is 1.30 – 2.30 p.m. This is in the afternoon.
b	1.15 p.m.	The timetable shows that lunch starts at 12 and finishes at 1.15 p.m.
c	Swimming	Swimming is from 2.45 – 3.30 p.m. 3 p.m. is during this time, so people are swimming at 3 p.m.

Focus

1 This timetable shows a day at the seaside for Iqra.

Arrive	Play games	Eat lunch	Walk	Swim	Leave
10.15 a.m.	11.15 a.m. – 12 p.m.	12.15 – 1 p.m.	1.30 – 2 p.m.	2 – 3 p.m.	3.15 p.m.

a What time did Iqra arrive? What time did she leave?

_____

_____

_____

b What was Iqra doing at 12.30 p.m.?

_____

c When did Iqra finish playing games?

_____

d Iqra's mum buys ice creams at 2.20 pm. Why is this a bad idea?

_____

2   This table shows the journeys of five short flights.

	Take-off	Landing
flight A	11:05	11:55
flight B	9:20	9:58
flight C	2:06	2:42
flight D	1:03	1:47
flight E	6:12	6:52

a   Piotyr's plane arrives back in his home town at 1.47.
    What flight is he on?

    _____

b   Anya arrives at the airport at 2:10. She has just missed her flight.
    Which flight was she supposed to be on?

    _____

c   Valerie arrives at the airport at 1:30. Which is the next flight?

    _____

3   Use the school timetable to answer the questions.

9:00–9:15	spelling
9:15–10:00	writing
10:15–11:00	maths
11:00–11:20	morning break
11:20–11:45	reading
12:00–12:45	science
12:45–1:00	break
1:00–1.30	lunch
1:30–2:00	music
2:00–3:00	art

a   At what time does the music lesson start?
    At what time does it finish?

    _____

    _____

b   At what time does maths start?
    At what time does maths finish?

    _____

    _____

c   By what time do you need to get to school in the morning?

    _____

d   On the timetable, what is your favourite lesson? When does it start?

    _____

Practice

4 This timetable shows the buses that go from the train station to the bus station each morning.

train station	9:06	10:05	12:00
shopping centre	9:21	10:23	12:18
school	9:35	–	12:32
park	9:48	10:40	–
bus station	10:00	10:59	12:50

a Kalpana missed the 9:21 bus from the shopping centre to school. What time is the next bus that she could catch?

_____

b What time is the last bus from the train station to the park? What time does the bus arrive?

_____

_____

c Use the information in this timetable to write a question and its answer.

_____

_____

_____

_____

_____

5 The timetable shows the times that it takes to travel between Elmswell and Norton, using different types of transport.

	Elmswell	Nacton	Daisy Green	Norton
bus	8:00	8:14	8:25	8:37
minibus	8:00	8:12	8:21	8:30
train	8:07	–	8:19	8:28

a You need to be at Norton before 8:30. Which transport would you use? What time would you arrive?

_____

b You miss the 8:12 minibus at Nacton to Daisy Green. What else could you use? What time would you arrive?

_____

6 This timetable shows the A14 bus route from the bus station to the train station.

bus station	6:05	7.10	9:00	10:10	12:05	1:05
High Road	6:15	7:18	9:15	10:30	12:20	1:20
shopping centre	6:34	7:36	9:30	10:45	12:34	1:34
village hall	6:48	7:50	9:40	–	12:50	1:50
train station	7:00	8:00	9:59	–	–	2:00

a What time does the first bus leave from the bus station?

_____

b When does it arrive at the village hall?

_____

c   If I want to get to the village hall before 8:00, which two buses can I catch from High Road?

_____

d   How many A14 buses stop at the village hall?

_____

Challenge

7   This timetable shows the B26 bus route from the bus station to the train station. Some rain has dropped onto the timetable and washed out the bus numbers.

bus station	9:00	11:05	2:00	4:30	6:05
High Road	9:10	11:15	2:05		6:10
shopping centre	9:25		2:10	4:55	6:25
village hall	9:50		2:15		6:35
train station	9:55		2:20		6:45

a   Add the bus numbers to the top row of the table using these clues.

• Bus 150A only stops at one destination after the bus station.

• Bus 90E arrives at the village hall at twenty-five to seven.

• Bus 380 is the first bus to leave the bus station in the morning.

• Mia uses Bus 222 to arrive at the train station for the 2:30 train.

• Bus 3C is the bus that is left over.

8   Use the timetable to answer the questions.

Bus timetable					
Oakham	6:00	6:30	7:10	7:13	8:12
Beedwell	6:10	6:40	–	7:29	8:28
Stumpy Well	6:14	6:44	7:18	7:34	8:31
Ironside	6:23	6:50	7:23	–	–
West Hall	6:28	6:55	7:28	7:51	8:45
Matchwell	6:35	7:00	7:43	7:59	9:00

a   Can you travel from Oakham to Ironside on the 7:13 bus?

_____

b   If you had to travel from Oakham to West Hall and had
    to arrive by 7:30, which would be the best bus to catch?

_____

c   The 6:40 bus from Beedwell is full. You need to arrive at
    Matchwell by 8:00. Can you still do this?
    How would you get there?

_____

9 The teacher from class 3 has made a timetable of
   school activities.

Monday		Tuesday		Wednesday		Thursday	
3:00–4:00	cycling	2:00–3:00	Jujitsu	2:00–3:00	gardening	3:00–4:00	cooking
3:15–4:00	gardening	3:00–4:00	drama	3:00–4:00	football	3:00–3:45	French
		3:00–4:00	singing	4:00–5:00	computer studies	3:00–4:00	arts & crafts
		4:15–5:00	arts & crafts			4:00–5:00	dodgeball

Li-Ming wishes to go to arts and crafts, cooking,
gardening and cycling. Make a list for Li-Ming of the
days and times that she can do her activities.

_____

_____

_____

_____

_____

15 > Angles and movement

> 15.1 Angles, direction, position and movement

cardinal point
compass
right angle

Exercise 15.1

Worked example 1

Draw a (ring) around all the angles that are not right angles.

Use your angle measure to help you.

How do you know the angles you have ringed are not right angles?

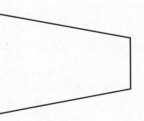
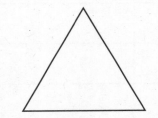

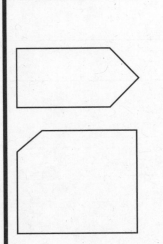

Continued

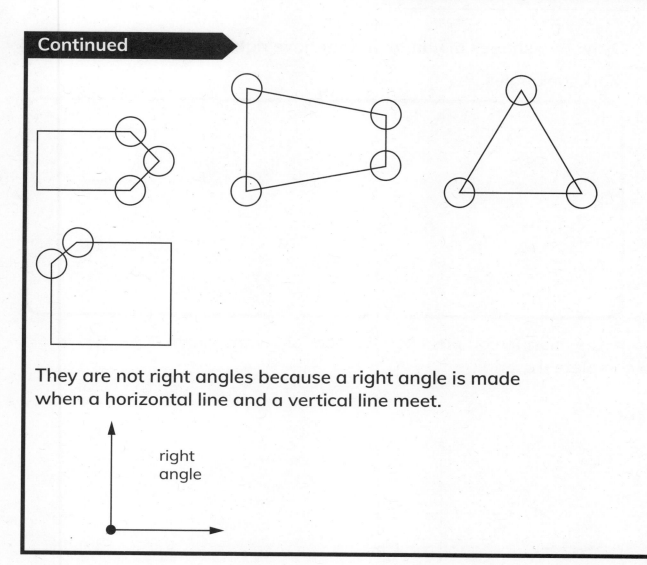

They are not right angles because a right angle is made when a horizontal line and a vertical line meet.

right angle

Focus

1 a Put a (ring) around all the right angles inside the shapes.

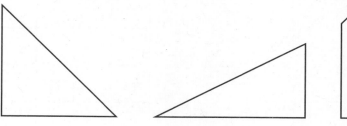
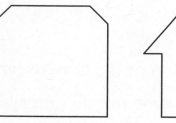

b   Draw two shapes of your own that have right angles.

Mark the angles.

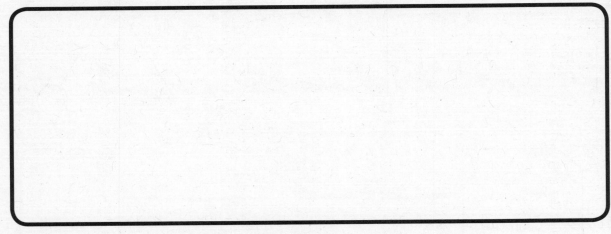

2   Write the missing compass points, then follow the clues
to complete the grid.

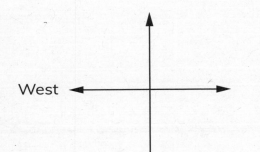

West

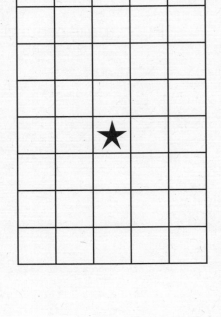

Starting at the star, draw:

- a green circle four spaces north

- a blue circle three spaces south

- a yellow circle two spaces west

- a red circle one space east.

3 On each side of the grid, write the missing cardinal points.

Complete the sentences.

Tree	Castle	School
Pond	Tent	Bridge
Park	Fire station	House

a The tree is _____ of the castle and _____ of the pond.

b The school is _____ of the castle and _____ of the bridge.

c The park is _____ of the pond and _____ of the fire station.

d The tent is _____ of the castle and _____ of the fire station and

_____ of the pond and _____ of the bridge.

e Where is the house?

_____

_____

Practice

4 Some of these shapes have right angles, some are greater than a right angle and some are less than a right angle.

Join one of the angles from each shape to the correct words.

right angle   less than a right angle   greater than a right angle

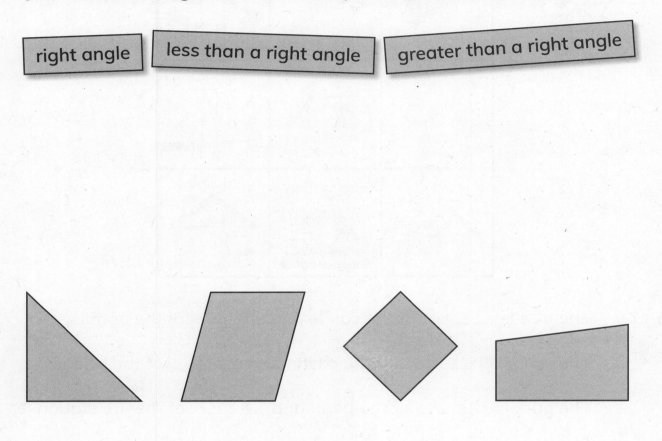

5

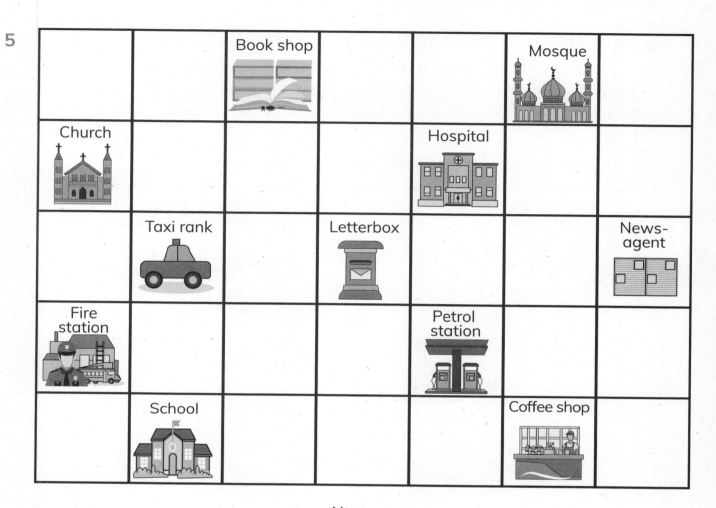

		Book shop			Mosque	
	Church				Hospital		Mosque
		Taxi rank		Letterbox			News-agent
	Fire station				Petrol station		
		School				Coffee shop	

Write two different sets of instructions to get from the school to the hospital.

1 _____

_____

2 _____

_____

6   Fill the map to show these objects: a tree, a pond, a pot
    of gold, some bushes, a river with a bridge and a person.

> **Tip**
>
> A compass can point in any direction, but remember that
> the cardinal point must always follow the same order.

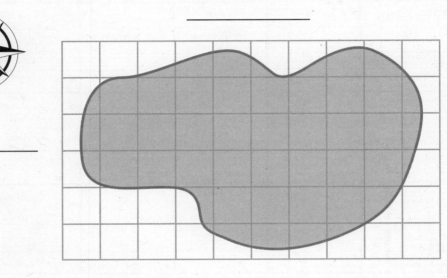

a   Write the four cardinal points.

b   Write two sentences to describe the position of the objects
    on your map. Use two cardinal points for each sentence.

    For example: The tree is west of the bridge and south
    of the pot of gold.

    1   _____

    2   _____

Challenge

7   a   Draw a (ring) around the angles that are greater than
        a right angle.

    b   Cross through the angles that are less than a right angle.

    c   Explain what this angle is and how it is made.

_____

_____

8

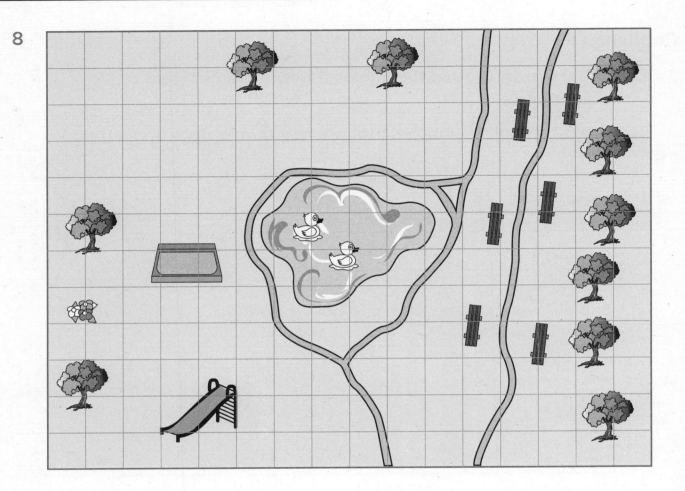

Using the cardinal points north, south, east and west,
write the position of six things on the map.

_____

_____

_____

_____

_____

_____

9

a   Write the missing words.

The _____ is west of the treasure box.

The hut is _____ of the treasure box.

b   Where are the mountains?

_____

c   Where is the ship?

_____

d   Walk from the tree towards the ship. In which direction
    will you walk?

_____

e   Add two more objects to the map. Write instructions to get to the two objects, starting from the tree.

Use all four cardinal points for each object.

_____

_____

_____

_____

16 Chance

> ## 16.1 Chance

Exercise 16.1

Worked example 1

a What is the chance of the spinner landing on black?

b Does it have more chance of landing on grey?

c Are you more likely to land on white or a shaded space (grey or black)?

chance
likely
might happen
will happen
will not happen

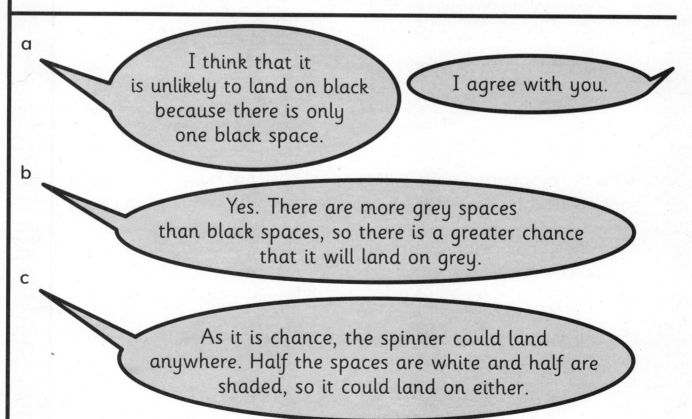

a I think that it is unlikely to land on black because there is only one black space.

I agree with you.

b Yes. There are more grey spaces than black spaces, so there is a greater chance that it will land on grey.

c As it is chance, the spinner could land anywhere. Half the spaces are white and half are shaded, so it could land on either.

Focus

1 a Draw a (ring) around your answer.

I think it is **likely / unlikely** that the spinner will land on red.

Why do you think that?

_____

_____

_____

_____

b Draw a (ring) around your answer.

I think that the spinner **will land / will not land** on green.

Why do you think that?

_____

_____

2 Read the problems. Write 'will happen', 'will not happen' or 'might happen' next to each one.

You will help a partner with their work next week. _____

You will go home on a bus after school tomorrow. _____

You will see a lion on your way home from school today.

_____

You will go to the shop tomorrow. _____

3   Play this game.

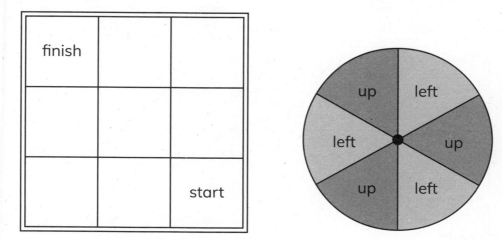

You will need to use the spinner.

Place a counter on 'start'. Spin the spinner.

The spinner tells you the direction to move your counter.

Move one square in that direction. If there is no space, stay where you are until your next turn.

a   How many times did you need to spin the spinner before you got to 'finish'?

_____

b   Will that always happen?

_____

_____

Practice

4   The spinner will land on yellow.

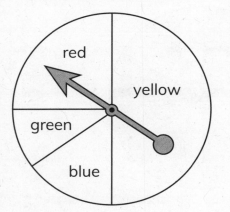

Do you agree? What do you think and why?

_____

_____

5   Write one sentence for each question.

a   This will happen:

_____

b   This might happen:

_____

c   This will not happen:

_____

6 You will need a coin and a paperclip for the spinner.

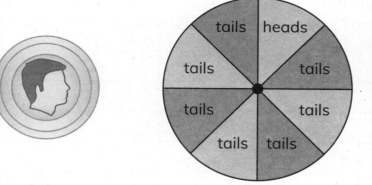

a Do you think you are more likely to land showing 'heads' on the coin or the spinner? Explain your thoughts.

_____

_____

b Toss the coin five times. Record your results in the table by ticking (✓) the correct box for each toss.

Coin toss	Heads	Not heads
Toss 1		
Toss 2		
Toss 3		
Toss 4		
Toss 5		

Spin the spinner five times. Record your results in the table by ticking (✓) the correct box for each spin.

Spin	Heads	Not heads
Spin 1		
Spin 2		
Spin 3		
Spin 4		
Spin 5		

c   What do your results show? Do they match what you thought would happen? Explain your answer.

_____

_____

Challenge

7   Write two questions for your partner that link with these pictures. Use the word 'chance'.

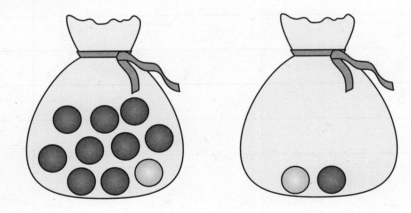

1 _____

_____

2 _____

_____

8 a If you roll a 1 to 6 dice without looking, how likely is it that you will get a 7?

| will happen | will not happen | may happen |

b Write dice questions that have the answers 'will happen' and 'will not happen'.

_____

_____

_____

9 Zara and Marcus have each made a spinner.

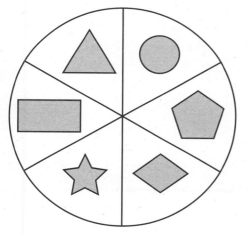

Zara's spinner

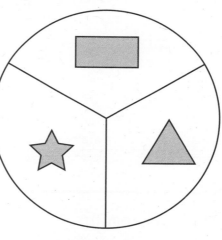

Marcus's spinner

If we each spin our spinners ten times, I think that I will land on the star more times than Zara.

a   Do you agree with Marcus's conjecture? Explain your answer.

_____

_____

b   Use a paperclip and pencil to carry out the experiment.
    Record your results below.

c   Describe your results.

_____

_____

17 ▶ Pattern and symmetry

› 17.1 Shape and symmetry

Exercise 17.1

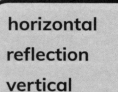
Worked example 1

Each flag has zero, one or two lines of symmetry.

Draw the vertical and horizontal lines of symmetry on each flag. Write how many lines you found.

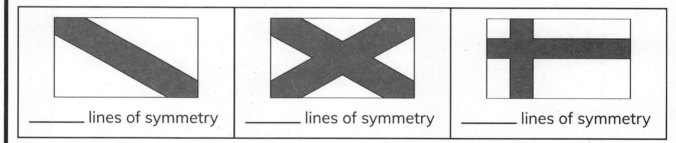

_____ lines of symmetry   _____ lines of symmetry   _____ lines of symmetry

If a shape has symmetry, both sides will be the same. Flag 1 does not have horizontal or vertical symmetry. Flag 2 has one vertical and one horizontal line of symmetry. Flag 3 has no lines of symmetry.

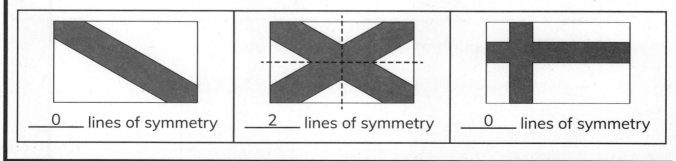

__0__ lines of symmetry   __2__ lines of symmetry   __0__ lines of symmetry

Focus

1   Each flag has zero, one or two lines of symmetry.

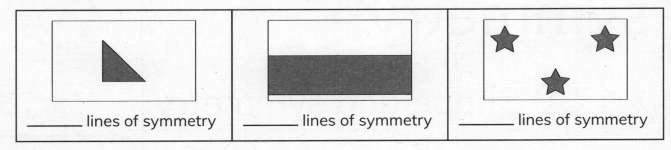

_____ lines of symmetry   _____ lines of symmetry   _____ lines of symmetry

a   Draw the vertical or horizontal lines of symmetry
    on each flag.

b   Write how many lines you found.

c   Draw two flags: one has one line of symmetry and
    one has two lines of symmetry.

2   a   Draw the reflection of each of these shapes.

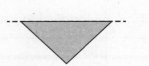 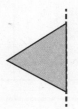

b Draw two shapes of your own. Draw any lines of
   symmetry that you can see.

3 a Draw the lines of symmetry in these shapes. Use a ruler.

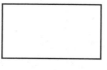 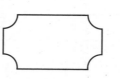

b Draw two lines of symmetry in these patterns.

c Draw your own symmetrical patterns.

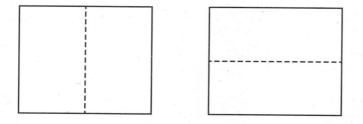

Practice

4   Each flag has zero, one or two lines of symmetry.

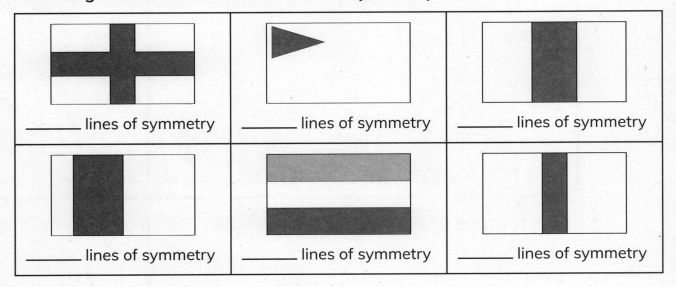

a   Draw the vertical or horizontal lines of symmetry
     on each flag. Write how many lines you found.

b   Where a flag has zero lines of symmetry, add to the flag
     the shapes that will give it one or two lines of symmetry.

     Draw the new vertical or horizontal lines on those flags.

5   a   These shapes were made by folding and cutting squares.

          Draw the lines of symmetry where you can.

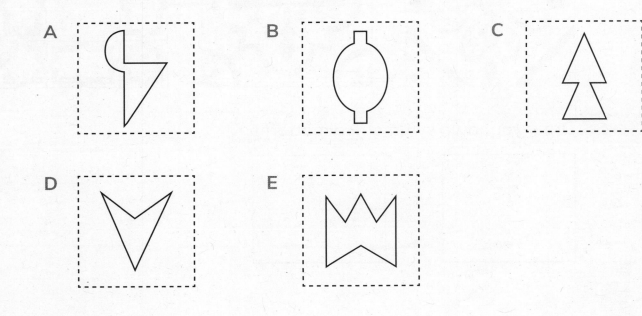

b Draw the reflection of this shape.

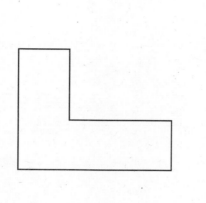

6 Draw the vertical or horizontal line of symmetry on this pattern. Use a ruler.

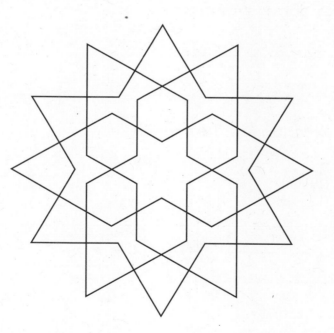

Colour the shape so that it keeps the line(s) of symmetry.

Challenge

7   Choose the shape for your flag.

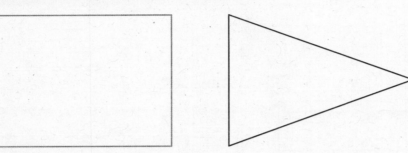

Draw your own design.

Create a symmetrical flag that has one or two lines of symmetry.

Use three different colours that are symmetrical too.

Draw the lines of symmetry on your flag.

Explain why they show symmetry.

_____

_____

8   a   Draw the reflections of the two shapes.

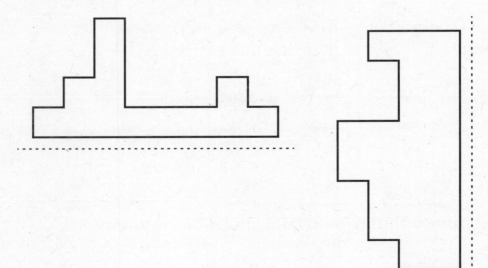

b   Draw two symmetrical shapes of your own that have
    two lines of symmetry. Mark the lines of symmetry.

9   This pattern has two lines of symmetry.

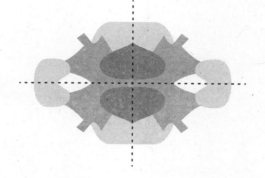

a   Label the vertical line. Label the horizontal line.

b   Using shapes, make your own pattern with two
    lines of symmetry. Colour it so that the colours
    are symmetrical.

> 17.2 Pattern and symmetry

Exercise 17.2

a constant	extend
shorten	symmetry

Worked example 2

Extend this pattern using a constant.

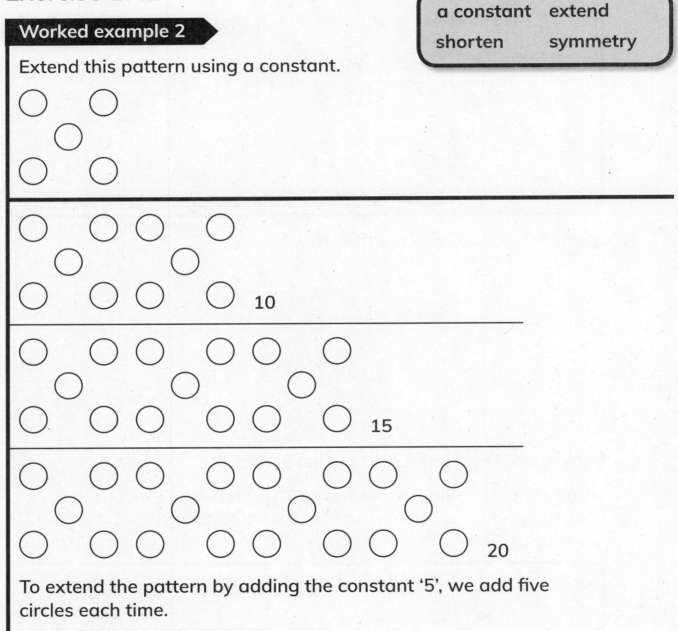

To extend the pattern by adding the constant '5', we add five circles each time.

This pattern goes up in five circles.

5, 10, 15

The next pattern will have 20 circles.

Focus

1 a Extend this pattern.

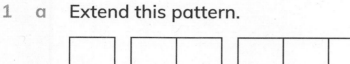

b The pattern goes up in _____.

2 This is the constant.

a Reduce this pattern by subtracting one constant at a time.

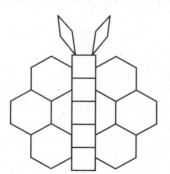   △

　　　　　4　　　　　_____　　　　_____　　　　1

b The pattern goes down in _____.

3 This pattern has one line of vertical symmetry.

Use colours to show colour symmetry.

Practice

4   This is the constant.

This is the starting pattern.

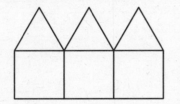

   a   Extend the pattern by one. Do this twice.

   b   Complete the number sentences.

        3   3 + 1 =   4 + 1 =

   c   Write one thing that you notice.

   _____

5   Make an extending pattern of your choice.

     This is my starting pattern:

     This is my constant:

     This is my extended pattern:

     Write one thing about your pattern to share with someone else.

   _____

6   a   Draw a picture or pattern with a horizontal line of
        symmetry to show reflection.

————————————

    b   How do you know that it is symmetrical?

_____

Challenge

7   Make an extending pattern using a constant of three different shapes.

    This is my starting pattern:

    This is my constant:

    This is my extended pattern:

    Write the total number of shapes below each extended pattern.

    Write one thing about your pattern to share with someone else.

_____

8   Make a pattern that reduces by one constant each time.

This is my starting pattern:

This is my constant:

This is my extended pattern:

Write the total number of shapes below each pattern.

Write one thing about your pattern to share with someone else.

_____

9   a   Draw a picture or pattern to show vertical and horizontal symmetry.

b   Where did you start?

_____

c   Explain what you did.

_____

_____

> Acknowledgements

It takes an extraordinary number of people to put together a new series of resources, and their comments, support and encouragement have been really important to us. We would like to thank the following people: Phillip Rees and Veronica Wastell for the support they have given the authors; Lynne McClure for her feedback and comments on early sections of the manuscript; Thomas Carter, Caroline Walton, Laura Collins, Charlotte Griggs, Gabby Martin, Elizabeth Scurfield, Berenice Howard-Smith, Zohir Naciri, Emma McCrea and Eddie Rippeth as part of the team at Cambridge preparing the resources. We would also like to particularly thank all of the anonymous reviewers for their time and comments on the manuscript and as part of the endorsement process.

The authors and publishers acknowledge the following sources of copyright material and are grateful for the permissions granted. While every effort has been made, it has not always been possible to identify the sources of all the material used, or to trace all copyright holders. If any omissions are brought to our notice, we will be happy to include the appropriate acknowledgements on reprinting.

Thanks to the following for permission to reproduce images:

Cover Photo: Pablo Gallego (Beehive Illustration)

Jan Hakan Dahlstrom/Getty Images; Juan Silva/Getty Images; Paapa Kwasi Gyamfi-Aidoo / EyeEm/Getty Images; Karl Hendon/Getty Images; Mohd Hafiez Mohd Razali / EyeEm/Getty Images; Tiina & Geir/Getty Images; Hsing-Yi Su / EyeEm/Getty Images; filo/Getty Images; Liyao Xie/Getty Images; MirageC/ Getty Images; maurizio siani/Getty Images; Cocoon/Getty Images; Liyao Xie/ Getty Images; Liu Chi San / EyeEm/Getty Images; Volanthevist/Getty Images; AHS Photography – Alex Schregardus/Getty Images; ARUTTHAPHON POOLSAWASD/Getty Images; Anawat Sudchanham / EyeEm/Getty Images; Kyle Chmielewski / EyeEm/Getty Images; Tim Grist Photography/Getty Images; Alex Schregardus/Getty Images; Marco Guidi/EyeEm/Getty Images; Valentin Valkov/500px/Getty Images; borchee/Getty Images.